THE
FINANCIAL
ACTIVIST
PLAYBOOK

8 STRATEGIES FOR EVERYDAY PEOPLE TO RECLAIM WEALTH AND COLLECTIVE WELL-BEING

JASMINE RASHID

BK
Berrett–Koehler Publishers, Inc.

Berrett-Koehler Publishers, Inc.
1333 Broadway, Suite P100
Oakland, CA 94612-1921
Tel: (510) 817-2277
Fax: (510) 817-2278
bkconnection.com

ORDERING INFORMATION

Quantity sales. Special discounts are available on quantity purchases by corporations, associations, and others. For details, please go to bkconnection.com to see our bulk discounts or contact *bookorders@bkpub.com* for more information.

Individual sales. Berrett-Koehler publications are available through most bookstores. They can also be ordered directly from Berrett-Koehler: Tel: (800) 929-2929; Fax: (802) 864-7626; *bkconnection.com.*

Orders for college textbook/course adoption use. Please contact Berrett-Koehler: Tel: (800) 929-2929; Fax: (802) 864-7626.

Distributed to the US trade and internationally by Penguin Random House Publisher Services.

Berrett-Koehler and the BK logo are registered trademarks of Berrett-Koehler Publishers, Inc.

Printed in Canada

Berrett-Koehler books are printed on long-lasting acid-free paper. When it is available, we choose paper that has been manufactured by environmentally responsible processes. These may include using trees grown in sustainable forests, incorporating recycled paper, minimizing chlorine in bleaching, or recycling the energy produced at the paper mill.

Library of Congress Cataloging-in-Publication Data
Names: Rashid, Jasmine, author.
Title: The financial activist playbook : 8 strategies for everyday people to reclaim wealth and
    collective well-being / Jasmine Rashid.
Description: First edition. | Oakland, CA : Berrett-Koehler Publishers, Inc., [2024] | Includes
    bibliographical references and index.
Identifiers: LCCN 2024004800 (print) | LCCN 2024004801 (ebook) | ISBN
    9781523006366 (paperback) | ISBN 9781523006373 (pdf) | ISBN 9781523006380 (epub)
Subjects: LCSH: Financial planners. | Finance, Personal.
Classification: LCC HG179.5 .R37 2024 (print) | LCC HG179.5 (ebook) | DDC
    332.024—dc23/eng/20240506
LC record available at https://lccn.loc.gov/2024004800
LC ebook record available at https://lccn.loc.gov/2024004801

First Edition

32 31 30 29 28 27 26 25 24   10 9 8 7 6 5 4 3 2 1

Book producer and text designer: Happenstance Type-O-Rama
Cover design: Ashley Ingram

For those reimagining the flow of money
and peace—from Dhaka to Detroit, West Papua
to Palestine, and every stunningly underestimated
corner of our wild wealth-full world.

CONTENTS

INTRODUCTION
Who's a Financial Activist?

The most common way people give up
their power is by thinking they don't have any.

—ALICE WALKER, author, poet, and social activist[1]

The financial activist is curious. They want to know how it feels to live in a society where everyone moves from a place of joy and abundance rather than a place of frustration and scarcity.

The financial activist is practical. They recognize that no one can do everything, but everyone can do something.

The financial activist is ready. Ready to reclaim wealth that's been stolen and stop pretending that our current financial system is the best we can do. Ready to show up and just start *somewhere*, even in the busyness of modern life. And ready to collaborate with others, repurposing money and finance for community wealth building and well-being.

There's a good chance the financial activist is you.

It's possible you picked up this book because you're excited by the prospect of gaining some clarity and being able to visualize the networks of wealth all around you. Or maybe someone lovingly gifted you this book, because they see how you're already subverting "business as usual" and helping co-create the next, more just economy. And if you made it this far, I'm willing to bet that you're here to see us all win.

So first—notice how the term *financial activist* lands with you. Does it feel like an oxymoron? Excite you? Bore you? Maybe even scare you a little? There's no right answer. Depending on your lived experience, both finance and activism can feel "way over there" (like in corporate-y skyscrapers and bustling street protests, respectively).

In the simplest terms, a **FINANCIAL ACTIVIST*** refers to anyone intentionally taking action in ways big and small to shift the flow of capital and power, resisting systems that cause harm to people and the planet for the sake of profit, and redesigning our relationships to money and one another.

Financial activists are explicitly working to reverse the prevailing financial trends of the 2020s, which, according to the International Monetary Fund, can be summarized as increasing financial uncertainty, increasing financial instability, and increasing financial inequality for everyday people.[2] In other words, financial activists are doing the work of ensuring we all experience more security, stability, and opportunities to thrive.

At the individual level, this work might look like getting to a place of personal financial ease—putting food on the table tonight and disrupting cycles of scarcity for generations to come. At the collective level, this work might look like big organizing to change **CAMPAIGN FINANCE** laws, raise worker **WAGES** across industries, or increase investments into **SOCIAL ENTERPRISES**.

All of our actions are interconnected. And with all the work there is to do in creating a more just economy, no form of financial activism is inherently more worthwhile than another. If we want an economy that truly works for everyone, we'll need everyone's contributions in the process.

Let's Peoplewatch

Picture this: we're at a suburban mall or a city street fair (your choice) in MostAnyTown, USA. We decide to grab a seat, each minute observing at least one stranger. Passersby include the following:

- ◉ A **grocery store cashier** who opened a savings account at the local **CREDIT UNION** last week and is explaining the benefits to her coworker.

---

* Key terms appear in all capitals throughout the book as well as in the online glossary at *JasmineRashid.com.*

- A **group of college friends** buying their favorite snacks to bring to tonight's monthly gathering, where they plot how to reach their financial goals.

- An **up-and-coming artist** who bartends to pay the bills and uses art to draw awareness to the billions in TAXPAYER DOLLARS being used to fund violence abroad.

- A **family of nurses and medical technicians** who are vocal about their firsthand experiences of why we need fair drug pricing and universal access to quality healthcare, like, yesterday.

- A **teacher** who helps students connect history lessons, the financial system, and what they as youth may experience daily heading to and from school.

- A **sixteen-year-old** who can't yet vote in official elections but has some pretty damn good ideas about what the community center needs for the upcoming town budget review.

- A **content creator** who isn't afraid to call out the absurdity of housing prices and knows that, no, the problem isn't that millennials just spend all their money on avocado toast.

- A **software engineer** who donates 5 percent of her income to GRASSROOTS advocacy groups, invests her savings in SOCIALLY RESPONSIBLE FUNDS, runs yoga classes with a SLIDING SCALE MODEL, and regularly sends money home to relatives abroad.

All these hypothetical strangers are financial activists.

Over the course of these pages, you'll meet and get personal with some real financial activists from all walks of life who are radically demonstrating how we transform finance for good in real time. They're WORKING CLASS, MIDDLE CLASS, women, queer folks, people of color, immigrants, and others who have for too long been underestimated and undervalued by dominant power structures. Collectively, their stories offer us a treasure trove of insights and inspiration: you'll learn not only what they do and how they do it, but also what underpins their daily commitment to supporting a more just economy.

These financial activists may not all be millionaires, but all are unquestionably wealthy: in relationships, wisdom, and reasons to be motivated. And many of them prove that *you don't have to have a ton of money right now to influence a ton of money right now.*

What's more, everyone I've interviewed for this book possesses perspectives that can't be learned in even the fanciest business school programs. They are each expert in their own unique lived experience.

The same goes for you.

We Need Your Expertise

Those on the frontlines of social change know that *the people closest to the problems are also often the people closest to the solutions.* They're just not typically the people also closest to the money and power to enact said solutions. It's funny how that works.

So, financial activism is largely about *challenging the inequities built into our dominant financial system by democratizing who gets to decide how and where money flows,* because those first and worst affected by issues like poverty are often the same people affected by issues of poor healthcare, pollution, policy failures, and so on.

Let's be real: there aren't some ultra-generous, all-knowing billionaires who are going to swoop in and solve the climate crisis or close this colossal wealth gap. It wouldn't work. Individuals can't solve collective problems. Instead, for lasting INTERSECTIONAL change to longstanding intersectional challenges, we need activism informed by hood politics and ancestral wisdom and everyday life under modern CAPITALISM, from every vantage point.

And we need your expertise and imagination to help us get clear on what financial flourishing looks and feels like, both at the individual and collective level. Yes, I'm talking to you. I checked and there's no one even remotely close to your level of insight in the everyday story of you—like the nuanced ways that the presence (and absence) of money impacts you and yours.

I need you to trust me that you have more power than the game of traditional finance might have you assuming. If you stay open to that, this Playbook will be a more effective companion on the journey of unlocking ways to move big money, time and again. The mightiness of financial activism starts with believing *we deserve better*, and knowing a new world is already deep in motion.

Speaking of which, let's take a second to demystify both pieces of the phrase *financial activism*—and why I think it's a term worth explicitly using.

Finance

FINANCE just means we're dealing with the MOVEMENT OF MONEY and the FUNDING OF THINGS AND PEOPLE. It's a big system encompassing personal money stuff, corporate money stuff, and governmental money stuff.

In North America in particular, many people can point to the traditional financial system as a vehicle for

- ⊙ ECONOMIC GROWTH—providing funding to businesses that create more jobs;
- ⊙ WEALTH CREATION—allowing individuals to invest in assets that grow over time; and
- ⊙ access to CREDIT—giving people borrowed money to purchase homes, cars, and other goods and services.

At the same time, it's been designed as a system for

- ⊙ extreme rising INEQUITY—prioritizing those with existing wealth to accumulate more wealth;
- ⊙ social and ENVIRONMENTAL DEVASTATION—supercharging industries and companies that damage the planet and engage in unethical practices; and
- ⊙ unending FINANCIAL CRISES—the Great Depression of the 1930s, the Great Recession of 2008, and the daily realities of way too many people today, for starters.

Across the world, our financial systems were designed by and continue to serve mostly wealthy white men, with a narrow focus on maximizing profits regardless of social and environmental impacts. Male. Pale. Stale.

So, business-as-usual-finance is stocks, it's bonds, it's calls to "buy low, sell high." It's a game that has helped some people achieve their wildest dreams and a gift that keeps on giving for generations to come. It's *Wolf of Wall Street* yacht glamour, retirement account boringness, and the strategies your one cousin swears by for being able to take a nice vacation every year.

And—not *or*—it's a system designed for and dredged in the lasting impacts of the slave trade, land theft, war profiteering, crushing debt, and mind-blowingly human-engineered inequality. It's the income we may be grinding countless hours a week to sustain ourselves with on one hand, while feeling bad about participating in a rigged system on the other, all while rightfully taking pride when we see the numbers in our bank account go up. The big world of our financial system shows up in intimate ways in our daily lives, and we're all allowed to claim just how personal and messy that can be.

That's finance.

Activism

As a catch-all term, *activism* is when people come together to challenge designed inequalities, corruption, and injustice—and help build a more fair, just, and SUSTAINABLE world—through public demonstrations, direct actions, or other forms of resistance. Think about how many of us come from lineages and homes where advocating for self and others has been an essential part of everyday life and survival for . . . ever. These traditions of labor and visioning aren't typically branded as ACTIVISM compared to more public events like protests, yet they are always, always core to what's happening behind the scenes of any lasting social change movement.

Despite what the political right likes to derisively claim, activism in the context of SOCIAL JUSTICE MOVEMENTS doesn't work to vaguely "make everyone equal." The goal is to concretely expand SELF-DETERMINATION—who receives opportunities *as well as* who can provide opportunities to others—prioritizing communities that have been systematically robbed of agency and pathways to thrive.

Note that while activism and **ORGANIZING** are sometimes used interchangeably, activism tends to be more focused on raising awareness and challenging power structures through direct action, while organizing is the deeper, long-term work of building relationships within communities, identifying and developing leadership, and facilitating opportunities for people to engage in collective action—think labor organizing, electoral organizing, donor organizing, and other types of power building. Activism and organizing are both necessary and complement each other, often including elements like

- ◉ **CAMPAIGNS** (multifaceted, overarching plans to achieve a specific goal);

- ◉ **STRATEGIES** (the broad approaches to accomplish that goal); and

- ◉ **TACTICS** (the specific actions within a strategy to enact change).

In short, activism is just how we alchemize despair about conditions to then materially change those conditions.

All Together, Now!

Put together, financial activism looks like creatively moving dollars *out* of harmful consolidation and *toward* widespread well-being. Rather than leaving money and power on the table, it's the practice of reclaiming financial resources and tools in line with larger social, economic, and climate justice movements. It's relegating the exploitation part of wealth building to the past.

As you assess opportunities for change, you might ask: What's the bar for qualifying any positive-intentioned action involving money as "financial activism," and not just, well, a positive-intentioned action involving money? In general, financial activism is grounded in collective visions of change that go beyond our individual circumstances. We set intentions to contribute to a movement in some way, rather than simply ending at what "moves" someone emotionally or will just benefit them personally.

Blending finance and activism offers a way for everyday people to challenge the very premise of traditional finance and a culture of **GATE-KEEPING**: the idea that only *some* have the right to access, understand,

and shape how, why, and to whom money moves. It's no coincidence that the growing financial activist movement looks a lot more mela-nated and femme than your average college econ class. We're here, baby.

And we're here right on time. There's never been a moment riper in history for financial activism than now. As I write this, we're experiencing the beginning of what some are calling the **GREAT WEALTH TRANSFER**, in which baby boomers (who hold half of the US's $140 trillion-with-a-T in wealth) will transfer their assets to younger generations like Gen X, millennials, and Gen Z through inheritance over the next few decades.[3] This is a historic opportunity for big change, especially because for the first time in modern financial history *women*, not men, are set to emerge as the primary wealth holders in the economy.

Additionally, we're living in times of unprecedented opportunity for interconnectivity, technology, and updated cultural norms. Each day brings news of rapidly developing tech that can be harnessed for creating and sharing information (hello, TikTok, and whatever app is about to replace it in popularity). Younger generations are increasingly meme-ifying the hypocritical shortcomings of just "pull yourself up by your bootstraps" rhetoric and laughing out loud at its logical fallacies. Wealth inequality is on full display, and people are increasingly walking out of workplaces where business profit skyrocket, but wages stay low.

More and more of us aren't afraid to say collectively: "Enough. What's next?"

Reclaiming Wealth, with Joy

Why a financial activist playbook?

Playbooks take stock and spell out strategies and tactics to rely on in crunch time. They outline defensive plays (how we stop our opponents) and offensive plays (forward momentum) to secure wins. Those who have quietly (and not so quietly) normalized building their wealth off everyday people spend a lot of time strategizing how to stay in and expand their power. It's time we fight back with our own Playbook.

But it's not only about fighting back. We get to define the goals of financial activism in terms not only of what we're moving away from, but also of what we're moving toward and what we're welcoming in: a radical reimagining and harnessing of money as a tool of the people, approaching wealth building through a lens of expansiveness and inclusivity. We're choosing to transform and build beautiful communities, not just resist harmful systems.

It's important for me to note that we'll be talking about some serious stuff with some high stakes throughout this Playbook. For sure. But it's a *play*book and not a textbook—this is your invitation to play, to get your hands dirty, to cultivate lightness and ease alongside the hard work of change.

(Or as my elder Akaya Windwood reminds us, "Despair is so available that choosing joy is revolutionary. A joyful people are harder to oppress."[4] She's also adamant that if we can't find time to laugh and shake our bums while building new systems, she doesn't want any part of it. I concur.)

Look: all movements are made up of people. Plain and simple, silly and endlessly complex, people. As a movement participant supporting social, economic, and climate justice, caring for community looks like caring for yourself. *You get to tend to your own* FINANCIAL FLOURISHING *as a part of, not in conflict with, building the more equitable economy we deserve.*

Using the Playbook

Elements of each chapter include insights from everyday financial activists, interactive exercises and activities, and NOTABLE TERMS (which you might have noticed you've already been working your way through—nice job!).

For those who appreciate a good "choose your own adventure," feel free to explore as you see fit, whether that means reading this book linearly, toggling between a few strategies you already suspect you want to go deeper on, or closing your eyes and flipping until you land on a section that just feels *right*. There are no real rules here, after all. It's y(our) Playbook.

And while you can read through this whole book by yourself if you please, you may also quickly find that the strategies are ultimately more effective when shared, discussed, and tried with others. Not to mention more fun.

In **Part I**, we'll get grounded by finding our unique roles to play, envisioning the economy we're collectively building, and dispelling some potential myths about financial activism, so that you head into the strategies with confidence.

In **Part II**, I've attempted to synthesize and categorize how outsized wealth is typically accumulated in our financial system . . . and then translate how those strategies can be remixed to work for everyday people and help fundamentally reshape the playing field. We'll spend quality time with each of the eight strategies, as each has its own full chapter and will appear in concert with the others.

This book is far from comprehensive, but I hope it serves as a starting point, spark, or supplement for you and your journey of financial activism. There are trillions of dollars to reclaim from bad actors, and trillions of ways to make an impact.

And truthfully, the goal of this Playbook is not to convince you to completely restructure your life (though if that's what you decide, please let me know so I can root you on forever). The goal is to give you a range of options, demystify the different elements of movement participation, and encourage you to start by trying just *one* intentional financial action where you are.

With joy and strategy, let's move some big money together, shall we?

PART I

GROUNDING

the culture financial activism aims to shift

✗		✓
scarcity	⟶	abundance
gatekeeping	⟶	accessibility
greed	⟶	generosity
grinding	⟶	flowing
wealth hoarding	⟶	wealth spreading

Let's ground our financial activism in a collective vision for a more just economy.

CHAPTER 1

We Are the Ones
We've Been Waiting For

*This is our moment to act: a massive wealth transfer over the next
25 years will shift tens of trillions of dollars into the hands of a
generation eager to address existential challenges.*

—DEB NELSON, founder of the Just Economy Institute[1]

I n many ways, this Playbook is both a tool for and a love letter to the
underestimated players no one expects to influence how and where
money flows, fundamentally changing finance and its role in our
society.

From retired elders to mid-career construction workers to burgeon-
ing creatives, financial activists all over the world are shifting cashflows
and traditional toxic relationships with money so that we can all live
more freely. We're not responsible for the systems that got us here, but
we can choose to be accountable to one another, from the spreadsheets
to the streets.

I'll draw from my own positionality throughout the book because
I think it's important that we—as women, as people of color, as young
people, and anyone who might be counted out—own our own stories.
So here goes.

At the time of this writing, I just turned twenty-seven. I work a full-
time job as the Director of Impact at impact investing firm Candide
Group, I treat my pit bull and French bulldog a little too much like
children, and I love the Oakland, California, condo my partner and I

call home (despite the fact that I'm sitting on the floor because a ceiling leak recently rearranged our furniture setup—and by "recently," I mean months ago).

As a millennial/Gen Z cusp baby, I wasn't surprised to learn through my research that most Americans born between 1997 and 2004 view capitalism as a whole negatively.[2] To me, that discontent is good news: it opens portals for change.

My personal love story with "people power" deepened in the summer of 2018, when I fell into the work of organizing alongside hundreds of others under the coalition banner of #FamiliesBelongTogether as part of my work with Candide. The backdrop was loveless: Trump's anti-immigrant rhetoric rang over constant media coverage of chaos at our southern border with Mexico. Imagery of brown children in cages became unavoidable to the American masses. Everyday people were asking big questions like "How is this happening?" which led to other big questions like "Who's funding this mess?"

Financial activists knew who was funding this mess. Over 70 percent of migrants at the time were being detained in for-profit prisons (also referred to as *private prisons* or PRIVATELY OWNED prisons).[3] The business model was quite literally to make as much money as possible by locking up as many people as possible, for as long as possible.[4] The cages were corporations.

To connect these dots for everyone, activists started publicizing the fact that private prisons were receiving close to $1 billion a year in contracts from US Immigration and Customs Enforcement (ICE), or almost $2.8 million of taxpayer money a day.[5] As in, everyday people's taxpayer money. They also broke down the fact that private prisons were financially structured as real estate investment trusts (REITs), a tax-advantaged type of investment that required the prisons to distribute 90 percent of profits to shareholders, making them heavily reliant on bank credit lines.[6]

So, the banks were funding the migrant detention centers separating families. Who was funding the banks?

That's where everyday people came in. Namely, the majority of Americans with checking and savings accounts at big-name banks. On weekly CORPORATE ACCOUNTABILITY strategy calls with leaders from advocacy groups like MomsRising, Worth Rises, and Presente.org, we decided to support consumers—people with bank accounts—to start putting pressure on their banks to stop investing in private prisons with our cash.[7]

On Valentine's Day 2019, we physically delivered "love letters" to bank headquarters in the form of thousands of pages of PETITIONS, signed by over five hundred thousand bank customers, threatening to close their accounts and take their business elsewhere.[8] Outside the Wells Fargo San Francisco headquarters, we carried "break up with private prisons" signs in the form of broken hearts, while migrant moms who had recently been incarcerated in these for-profit detention centers bravely shared their harrowing stories, adorable kiddos in tow.[9]

At the same time on the East Coast, our coalition partners in New York showed up with a mariachi band, serenading songs of heartbreak outside the house of JPMorgan Chase executive Jamie Dimon.[10] Across the country, people joined in on DIRECT ACTIONS by going to their local bank branches in groups to demonstrate love for migrant families and make it known they disapproved of their bank's relationship investing in and profiting from private prisons and immigrant detention centers.

Additionally, coalition members experienced in the language of traditional finance set up calls with bank officials themselves. We played a lot of "insider baseball," getting the banks' human rights lawyers on the phone, referencing the unflattering financial documents that we gained access to, reminding them of the real cost of mounting reputational risks, and so on. Other coalition members spent time in Washington, DC, directly LOBBYING politicians to listen to their constituents and outlaw the use of private prisons. We sent bank executives a letter signed by investors we reached out to—collectively representing $2.9 billion in assets—expressing their concerns about the human rights violations and financial implications of the business dealings.[11]

After months of this organizing, news started to break.

"JPMorgan Chase . . . will no longer bank the private-prison industry."[12]   AMERICAN BANKER, MARCH 5, 2019

"[Wells Fargo] has fully exited its credit agreement with Core-Civic."[13]   IN THESE TIMES, MARCH 14, 2019

> "'We have decided to exit the relationships we have with companies providing prisoner and immigrant detention services for federal and state governments,' [. . . said] a Bank of America spokesperson."[14] *FOX BUSINESS*, JUNE 17, 2019

Other funding dominoes—SunTrust Banks Inc., BNP Paribas, Fifth Third Bancorp, Barclays, PNC—began to fall.[15] The stock prices of the two largest private prison operators, CoreCivic and GEO Group, reached record lows.[16] Credit rating systems downgraded private prison stock to "junk," and the prisons had to disclose their profit losses to investors, which lost them more partners and made them rely on more expensive forms of capital.[17] The vast majority of big-bank financing to private prisons—over $2 billion—dried up.[18]

Everyday people did that.

I had my first taste of large-scale financial activism and what's possible when we mobilize for change. Everyone had a part to play.

Play Your Part

There are some "day jobs" that clearly have potential to shape our money systems. Financial analysts and economists, lawyers and policy advocates, nonprofit directors, philanthropic workers, and more can be key players in our fights for change. However, these positions represent just a teeny-tiny fragment of places where financial activists, and people in general, find themselves.

According to a 2023 analysis, the top ten most common jobs for Americans (in order of most prevalent to least) are cashiers, food preparation workers, stocking associates, laborers, janitors, construction workers, bookkeepers, servers, medical assistants, and bartenders.[19] Younger generations can be found en masse in roles like web developers, market research analysts, healthcare workers, firefighters, and product managers.[20] Not only is there potential to influence the flow of money in line with the next economy in each of these positions, but international labor trends show that an increasing number of millennials and Gen Zers are likely to explore many positions, careers, and industries over the course of their lives.[21]

What does that tell us? People are identifying less and less with "what they do" and more with "how they live." In other words—the unique skillsets, personality traits, relationships, affinity groups, hobbies, and gifts that make up one's quality of life. Financial activism is a piece of that "how we live."

EXERCISE
Identify Your Role(s) in the Movement

The following examples show how certain skills and personality traits might translate to financial activism. *Do any of these sound like you or someone you're close to?*

◉ **You're a creative at heart.** Creativity is essential for breaking free from "business as usual," crafting out-of-the-box solutions, and drawing others into the fold.

◉ **You love playing detective and solving puzzles.** Money flowing behind the scenes can often be hard to suss out, and mystery lovers with an eye for detail help us lock down clues and reveal dark dealings lurking in the shadows.

◉ **You're resilient and understand life's ups and downs.** Finance can be a roller coaster, full of unpredictable highs and lows. The ability to keep it moving and grow from challenges is a skill you can't necessarily learn in the classroom.

◉ **You're a gifted storyteller.** Successful financial activism depends on more people being able to decode financial terminology and speak truth to power. Translating jargon into plain English (or Spanish, or Arabic, or Tagalog) is often step one for change.

◉ **You're emotionally intelligent and care deeply about others.** To prevent the burnout that too often plagues our social change movements, we need empaths to direct and sustain us in caring for ourselves and the whole.

⊙ **You're Marie Kondo–level organized.** The mass movement of people and dollars requires folks who can thoughtfully map out, color-coordinate, and rally the masses in line with strategies.

Our roles in social change can be fluid and change over time and circumstances, but often we just *know* what resonates with us when we see it in front of us. You know the feeling! To give it a try, I highly recommend checking out the Social Change Ecosystem framework developed by Deepa Iyer, described in her book *Social Change Now: A Guide for Reflection and Connection.*[22] It's a great resource for helping identify key roles—from disrupters to weavers, experimenters to caregivers—in community.

No one can do everything, everywhere, all at once. What might be *your role right now* in creating a more just economy?

_____

_____

Five Steps to Claiming Your Role as a Financial Activist

Among the financial activists who shared their success stories with me, a clear pattern emerged across even the widest of experiences. Participants first recalled early moments when they dared to ask questions others weren't asking (1). Then they opened up about how the challenge in front of them affected them on an emotional level (2). They imagined how things could be different (3), then started with a small money experiment of their own (4). Eventually, they found their way to connect with a larger community (5), and together they moved noteworthy amounts of money in unprecedented ways.

Let's take, for example, an interview I did with Sasheen Andregg, who begins by recalling January 2023, when she wasn't able to shake a feeling of darkness overshadowing the promise of a new year.[23]

Forty-five minutes away from her, in Half Moon Bay, California, seven migrant farmworkers had their lives abruptly stolen by another disgruntled employee with a gun, whose rage allegedly stemmed from a dispute over $100.

Sasheen found herself grief-googling. Her mind reached for any way she might be able to help. She remembered in the not-too-distant past seeing a news clip of the vice mayor of Half Moon Bay supporting a farmworker advocacy organization, so she found his contact info and emailed him for guidance. "Like, I feel bad if the vice mayor is getting inundated with emails," she laughs through tears, "but I need to know how to help because I'm not going to feel good in my soul if I'm not taking steps forward."

Hitting send on that first email catalyzed momentum for Sasheen. She found herself next writing a heartfelt letter to the executive sponsors of the employee resource group (ERG) she belonged to for people of Hispanic heritage at her midsize tech company. Here, she detailed the tragedies that had unfolded and shared that other coworkers within the company were also feeling rattled. She encouraged the executive sponsors to make a statement acknowledging the mass shootings and contribute financially to the Half Moon Bay victims' families.

To be clear, no one gave her permission to reach out to company leadership and make this ask. She just did it.

While there was some back-and-forth about legalities and logistics on the company's side, Sasheen ultimately convinced the executive sponsors to draft and publish a statement. And it didn't end there: a collective fundraiser was set up, inviting contributions from employees across the company's other ERGs. These contributions would be matched by corporate donations, unlocking much-needed funds for Ayudando Latinos a Soñar (ALAS), the Half Moon Bay–based nonprofit organization providing support to the victims, their families, and the local farmworker community at large. "Within the first week, we raised over $5,600. Which I know is a drop in the bucket, but it's a start and it's more than I would have been able to do just on my own as one person," Sasheen says.

Sasheen recognized the need for immediate financial support for survivors in the wake of the tragedy, *and* that support was needed long before the shootings and would be needed long after. For example, she knew about the harsh conditions these workers faced, and that they likely lived in overcrowded substandard housing with their children and families on site, where they toiled day in and day out.

"I'm a proud Chicana. . . . My grandparents were farm laborers from the time that they were young children. They were pulled out of grade school and made to work the fields," she shares. In other words, Sasheen knows who she is and whose she is.

The *San Francisco Chronicle* reported that the shootings exposed how the seven farmworkers and their families—twenty-seven people total—were housed by their employers in converted trailers with deplorable conditions.[24] And despite being the ones sustaining our food system, more than 60 percent of farmworkers reported having trouble paying for food since the pandemic hit, as detailed in the *LA Times* article aptly titled "Shooting Uncovers 'Plantation Mentality' in a Rich, Liberal California Enclave."[25]

In response to public exposés and financial activism like that of Sasheen and her coworkers, the farm employer has announced that they will build safer, permitted, and up-to-code housing for workers by next year.

"I hate giving presentations, I hate standing up and speaking in front of people, I'm not that person," Sasheen admits with a shy smile, "but it was still something like 'this needs to be done, this needs to be done.'"

Rather than receiving the backlash so many of us might fear when we choose to speak up in the workplace, Sasheen reflects on how her advocacy instead opened more doors to a larger community of people like her, who share values and dreams of a better society, and who now root for each other's success. "You attract what you put out," she reflects. "This idea of service is something we're all brought up with. You owe it to yourself and to others."

• • • •

Check this out.

As the descendant of migrant farmworkers, Sasheen connected the dots about the ways the shooting victims and their families were made vulnerable to violence and exploitation—questioning "Why is this like this?" (1). In trying to process the tragedy, she walked me through some of the raw, big emotions that came up for her, why it hit so close to home, and how she began sharing those feelings out loud with others—reckoning with "How do I feel about this?" (2). Of course, there's no one way to solve for issues as big as mass shootings. But in terms of addressing the real needs of those affected and ways she could work to make things even incrementally better from afar, Sasheen allowed herself to ask, "What's possible?" (3).

She felt motivated to just do *something*, which started with looking up the email address of the vice mayor of Half Moon Bay and writing to him to express her concern for the families, as well as her willingness to learn more about direct service groups to support—answering the question "What can I do right now?" (4). Then, she was ready to go bigger . . . and started brainstorming with people in her workplace about how they could collectively make a difference when they chose to address "What can we do together?" (5). The collective leveraged their unique access to corporate sponsors to unlock thousands in matching donor dollars for the victims and their families.

In each strategy chapter, I'll include signposts of these "five key steps to financial activism" (see Figure 1.1) to note where we are on the journey. Let's explore each step in more detail.

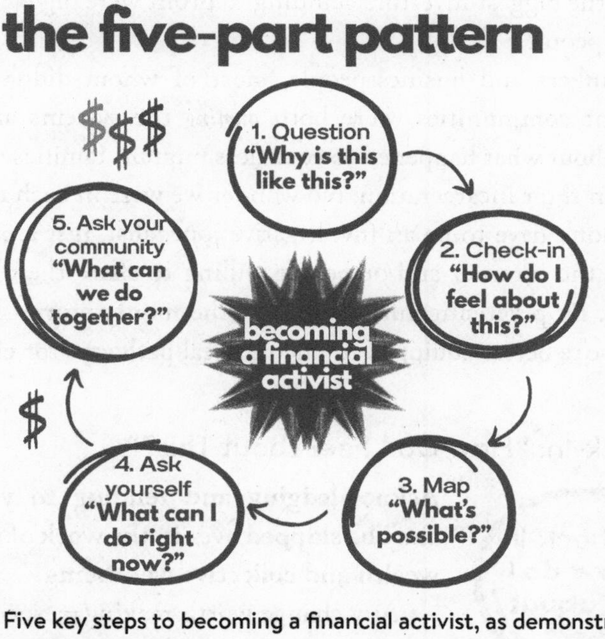

the five-part pattern

FIGURE 1.1. Five key steps to becoming a financial activist, as demonstrated by interviewees of this Playbook

1. Question: "Why Is This Like This?"

Bring a lens of curiosity to existing financial structures and practices, and uncover how money plays a role "behind the scenes" of any social issue.

When it comes to powering our visions of more flourishing communities, Nwamaka Agbo, the creator of the RESTORATIVE ECONOMICS Framework, reminds us that only community ownership plus community governance can give us true community self-determination—for political, cultural, and economic power.[26] In other words, we get to ask, "Who owns this?" and "Who makes decisions about this?" to better understand exactly who institutions, ideas, and innovations are designed to serve.

For example, recall the story I shared about the #FamiliesBelong-Together campaign to end the practice of family separation and abuses of detained migrants in private prisons. Activists dug deeper into the money story of how so many people were being detained in so many new privatized detention centers at so quick a pace. What they learned was that the biggest investors standing to profit were big banks used by everyday people.

So bankers and businesspeople, most of whom didn't hail from immigrant communities, were both *owning* the systems and making *decisions* about what happened to countless migrant families—and cashing out on their incarceration. No wonder we were in such a mess.

You don't have to be an investigative journalist, just a person with access to the internet and/or people willing to share their knowledge with you. By practicing curiosity about the money stories behind the stories, we're better equipped to uncover real pathways for change.

2. Check-In: "How Do I Feel about This?"

Acknowledging and tending to your needs can't be skipped over in the work of reclaiming wealth and collective well-being.

Any change worth making—especially when money is involved—can get uncomfortable.

Reclaiming power and joining movements for progress can be the highest forms of liberation, joy, and connection, but there's no use in pretending it's all sunshine and rainbows.

When I started getting involved in the movement to end family separation and private prisons, I felt . . . a lot. I remember my heart quickening with anger every time a headline about missing children and rampant abuse flashed on the TV. In other moments I felt very little—desensitized by the imagery of suffering, navigating personal life things, and so on.

I felt confused about how this was legal. I felt motivated to understand more. I felt frustrated at the people who refused to acknowledge America had a problem and instead took critique personally. I felt tired thinking about mass incarceration in general and its direct impact on people I know and love. I also felt a little powerless: we're talking big money, big political players, big systems—small brown girl in her early twenties.

There is no "fixing" hard feelings about hard things, there's only the practice of tending to them with consistency and without judgment. I know, I know, just acknowledging what's going on in your inner world may feel . . . what's the word? Woo-woo? Egotistical? A waste of precious time? But the truth is, glossing over the work of feeling our feelings to just get straight to the tactical can be dangerous and cause unintended harm. When we're "triggered," or in a state of an activated fight-flight-or-freeze nervous system, we're not going to have the capacity to make the most informed decisions. We might even take that overwhelm that's been bubbling under the surface unfairly out on those around us. Not fun!

EXERCISE
Halt!

Even when it doesn't feel like it, the tools to care for ourselves and each other are endless (shout-out to my therapist). When I'm looking at something that needs to change but I'm feeling personally

---

stuck—hopeless, overwhelmed, resentful—I try to transform those feelings into fuel for more useful feelings, like inspiration, excitement, and motivation. One tool for covering my bases is the handy acronym HALT, which is to check:

- ⊚ Am I hungry?
- ⊚ Am I angry?
- ⊚ Am I lonely?
- ⊚ Am I tired?

If I answer yes to any of these, they're probably getting in the way, and I should *attend to those needs*, stat.

I bet you didn't think that an invitation to eat a nourishing meal or get a workout in or call your favorite person or take a nap would be on your financial activist to-do list, but here we are.

3. Map: "What's Possible?"

Begin to visualize the relevant networks of people, institutions, and resources you're connected to, and don't be afraid to imagine new ways and places for money to flow.

Allowing our brains permission to think from a place of abundance rather than scarcity isn't just liberating—it's strategic. Any successful change, whether it's buying a dream home for your family or transforming an entire financial system, requires multiple strategies working at once in different ways.

In my experience of what's possible, financial activism can mesh cold emails, Canva, and cast members of *Orange Is the New Black*. Let's rewind.

Have you heard the saying "It's not about what you know, but who you know"? Fresh out of college, I was looking for meaningful, paid work and feeling dismayed that I had an inbox full of job rejection emails instead of a Rolodex full of "connections." But wait—I just graduated college. That's technically a whole institution full of potential connections that a lot of people don't have the same privilege to access with just the click of a button.

So, I started looking through my alma mater Swarthmore College's alumni network, reading about people's work, and sending cold emails to those whose work I was interested in learning more about. I sent them genuine but brief notes detailing exactly what I found admirable about their work, a bit about myself, and what type of work I generally looked to support just in case they had ideas or advice. Without knowing it, I was leaning into this step of "mapping what's possible" for myself.

One of the people I emailed, Morgan Simon, saw that more than my fancy bachelor's degree I had built a personal website, where I shared some of my activism work and flexed my design skills (aka a free Canva account). Morgan knew I was passionate about the work she and her organization Candide Group were involved in as part of the #FamiliesBelongTogether coalition. She asked if I could provide some support for campaign actions, and eventually, join the Candide team full-time.

We created a website, called Real Money Moves (*RealMoneyMoves.org*), where we encouraged celebrities to publicly leverage their platforms and take a stance against investing in private prisons and immigrant detention centers. Through Morgan's years as an impact investor, author, and public speaker, she had a lot of connections. Those connections had a lot of connections. And before we knew it, we had an eclectic group of influencers volunteering to make educational content with us—from NFL player turned impact investor Derrick Morgan to actress Alysia Reiner from Netflix's popular prison comedy-drama *Orange Is the New Black*—all speaking out against private prisons.

This sidebar effort was just a fraction of the campaign to raise awareness and divest billions of dollars out of the private prison industry, but it exemplifies the kinds of collaborations that are possible when you allow yourself to get creative. Lay out all your options on the table.

4. Ask Yourself: "What Can I Do Right Now?"

Just start somewhere, experimenting with one action, to build the confidence to keep going.

"There's no wrong way to start," shares food activist Ali Berlow. "But not starting—now that's a mistake."[27] I find this simple reminder immensely helpful in my own life, whether it's in the context of tidying my living space or an opportunity to influence investments.

In our efforts to end private prison financing, many people who joined had never before participated in a campaign calling out big banks. Some showed up during their lunch break to protests outside bank headquarters within walking distance of their workplace. Others made the effort to show up but turned around because the police presence around the protests made them wary, as I heard from an undocumented friend. Thousands of others took less than a minute to sign the online petition calling for an end to family separation. All attempts to contribute were helpful to the movement.

I've noticed that sometimes we hesitate to act, or even just learn more about something, when financial systems are involved, because we're afraid of "messing things up." I've been there. And though the fear isn't always rational, it's easy to see where it comes from—few of us are told that we have the ability or know-how to figure out new ways to influence money and financial systems for our communities.

It's like going to the doctor with an unexplained pain in your leg. First, you get there and have "white coat syndrome," the phenomenon where patients have a blood pressure spike because of the psychological stress of simply being in the doctor's office and in pain. Then, if your doc checks it out and says, "Nah, there's nothing wrong with your leg," doesn't give you any suggestions to address the pain, and tells you to keep your blood pressure in check, chances are you wouldn't question their authority at that moment. You might just say thanks, sign out with the nice ladies at the front desk, and go home with your still-unexplained leg pain.

Fortunately, you'd have other options at this point. You can schedule an appointment with another doctor for a second opinion. You can try some DIY measures like heat or ice. You can experiment with some light stretching or foam rolling to see if your leg gets better or worse. You start small with what you're comfortable with—not performing literal surgery on yourself.

In financial systems and social issues, when those in power tell us "nothing to see here" but we know something needs improving, we have the ability to start small and experiment with what we're comfortable with. Whether it's taking ten minutes to do research, five minutes to share a petition with your group chat, or one minute to hit a "donate" button, it's a worthwhile place to start your journey. Momentum needs a starting point.

5. Ask Your Community: "What Can We Do Together?"

Find your people and co-organize, because the work of big change can't be done alone.

One mama can change the lives of her children and have a ripple effect for generations. Imagine what millions of mothers working together can do.

That's the type of magic that national grassroots organization MomsRising (and its Latinx program, MamásConPoder) is all about. As a key coalition partner in the financial activist campaign to end big-bank financing of prisons, the organization leveraged its membership of moms in almost every state in the country—across class and culture—to host simultaneous actions and share petitions, putting undeniable pressure on the banks complicit in family separation.

They helped us host weekly strategy calls, which were open to anyone in the coalition, whether they were a communications associate at a nonprofit partner or the executive director of a legal advocacy group. Here, creative synergies between those who had media contacts, those who could reach potential donors, those who shared their stories, and those who organized shareholders mutually reinforced the might of our collective efforts.

Remember: each of us is connected to more money than what's currently in our bank accounts, our wallets, or under our mattresses. While single actions can amount to worthwhile contributions, the real power of financial activism is found in groups. Find your people to co-inspire, reclaim wealth, and experience the sweetness of belonging with. You'll hold one another lovingly accountable for the long work of building the flourishing lives we each deserve to live.

CHAPTER 2

Going Deeper
What Financial
Activism Is (and Isn't)

If you have come to help me, you are wasting your time.
If you have come because your liberation is bound
up with mine, then let us work together.

—LILLA WATSON, Murri activist
from Queensland, Australia[1]

I f we wanna talk about change, we gotta talk about power.

POWER is multidimensional: broadly speaking, it shows up as economic, cultural, and political influence. While financial activism focuses specifically on shifting power related to money (economic), it must go hand in hand with changing hearts and minds (cultural) as well as changing who sits at decision-making tables (political).

But wait: What about the old saying "money is power"? As a research exercise, I asked friends and strangers—with zero context—one question: "When do you feel powerful?" Here were some of the responses:

- ◉ "When I lift really heavy weights at the gym."
- ◉ "When walking and listening to a really good song!"
- ◉ "When I'm on top of life, work, and home simultaneously."
- ◉ "When I stand up for myself."

⦿ "When my actions make a tangible and valuable difference to someone or something."

⦿ "When I'm playing soccer."

⦿ "When I go on strike with tens of thousands of academic workers."

⦿ "When someone sees me for who I really am."

No one said, "I feel powerful when I have money." Now, money is often a useful tool in helping control events, navigating uncertainty, or affording the conditions of many power-inducing scenarios. But that makes it a *component* of power, not power in and of itself. The same goes with sayings like "knowledge is power": what you do with that resource, under what context, makes all the difference.

Financial activism asks us to acknowledge, leverage, and shift power in its many forms.

ACTION
Claim When You Feel Powerful

Write about a time you recently felt powerful, and reflect on why that might be:

_____

_____

_____

_____

Ready to get your first official financial activist tool for your toolkit?

POWER MAPPING is a beloved practice used in all types of activism and organizing to identify the actors, institutions, and structures that have influence over a particular issue or system. Figure 2.1 shows what a simple power-mapping template could look like.[2]

blank power map

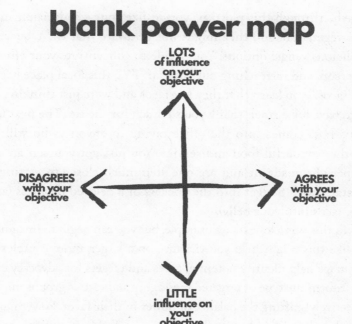

FIGURE 2.1. A power-mapping template

You can get as fancy as you like, but at its core, power mapping involves creating a visual representation of the power relationships and connections between different individuals and groups, which can help activists develop more effective strategies for social change.

Let's take a simple objective: you ask your organization to cater staff lunch from your favorite local family-owned taqueria that's been struggling to bring in new customers, instead of catering from Panera Bread (for the tenth time this year) and they say, "meh." On the power-mapping axes, you can plot the key decision-makers and resource-holders who are connected to the objective you're trying to reach, starting with the most influential figures, like the person who actually makes the lunch decision and the person who puts in the order. Assuming they're in the top-left quadrant (lots of influence, disagree with your objective), you then start plotting their key relationships with arrows—their office besties, their bosses, coworkers who might be sympathetic to your cause, and so on.

Maybe through this plotting, you realize your key decision-maker's boss is vegetarian, and they might not be aware that the taqueria also has delicious veggie options. You decide to concentrate your efforts on that person, and in reaching out with an "FYI, this local place has great veggie tacos!" you learn that they *love* tacos and were just thinking about what to have for dinner; thank you so much for the tip. The next morning this boss comes into the office raving to anyone who will listen about the wonderful food and service. You just got yourself an ally in the top-right quadrant and are one step much closer to getting your $500 staff lunch budget into the pockets of a beloved business (and, of course, tacos into your belly).

Okay, this was a low-stakes example, but you can begin to imagine how a tool like this might help you visualize on a larger, more complex scale. Power maps help identify potential allies and targets for advocacy efforts, which inform the type of targeted messaging and tactics groups might use for effectively shifting the balance of power in their favor. Power mapping can also be a lot of fun, but it takes practice, so feel free to start small.

Financial Activism Means Moving from Extraction to Regeneration

Since the first European settlers set up shop on what we now call the United States, we've operated under an economic system called RACIAL CAPITALISM.[3] A concept brought to public consciousness by Black studies great Cedric Robinson in the 1980s, *racial capitalism* is a system in which racial oppression and financial exploitation interconnect and reinforce each other in order for the wheels of the financial system to keep turning—from founding pillars of colonialism and slavery all the way through enduring dynamics of healthcare, criminal justice, and education disparities we know all too well today.

Financial activism propels us to move from an extractive racial capitalist economy (think inevitable combustion into violence and flames) to a regenerative economy (which can adapt and live on until the end of time). The wisdom of frontline communities and leaders, stewarded by the organization Movement Generation, informs the breakdown shown in Table 2.1.[4]

TABLE 2.1. Moving from an extractive economy to a regenerative one (adapted with permission from Movement Generation)

An EXTRACTIVE ECONOMY is an economy...	A REGENERATIVE ECONOMY is an economy...
✗ Whose **purpose** is to **enclose wealth and power**	✓ Whose **purpose** is to **promote ecological and social well-being**
✗ Where **work** is **exploitative**	✓ Where **work** is **cooperative**
✗ In which **resources** are **extracted** (dug up, burned, dumped)	✓ In which **resources** are **regenerated**
✗ Whose **governance** prioritizes **militarism**	✓ Whose **governance** prioritizes **deep democracy**
✗ Premised on a **worldview** of **consumerism and colonial mindsets**	✓ Premised on a **worldview** of **caring and sacredness**

On a related note, friends at the Capital Institute offer that we'll know we're operating in a state of regeneration when we, as individuals and communities,

- feel we're in **right relationship** with and deeply connected to others (humans and otherwise);

- truly view **wealth holistically**, beyond just money in the bank;

- can **innovate, adapt, and respond** to big changes;

- are in communities where everyone is **empowered to participate**, advocating for their own needs and contributing their unique gifts;

- **honor place and community**, informed by our unique histories and cultures;

- have **abundance at the "edges"** of our communities, not just in the centers;

- experience a **robust circulation** of money, information, and resources; and

- prioritize **balance.**[5]

(Emphasis my own.)

EXERCISE
Regeneration, Right Now

In your life, do you *already* experience elements of the "regeneration" list? (I invite you to read through the list again with this question in mind.)

_____

_____

_____

_____

Perhaps you come from a family that's helped you through an unexpected big life event. Or you recognize your partner's wealth as not just their income but the value they bring to your life. Or you're able to joyfully treat your best friend to a nice dinner and know that money will come back to you in one way or another. Or you find yourself working for an employer who knows your job isn't (and shouldn't consume) your whole life, so you get to leave work at work, for real though.

I bring this up because while sometimes these frameworks and principles can feel theoretical and intimidating, the truth is that many of us *already know* what it's like to live in a better economy, even in small ways. It's at our fingertips and, in some cases, already in our embrace. These revelations within our personal lives should give us hope about the cooperation, care, and ease we're capable of.

The same can be seen at societal levels. For example, the fact that hourly employees must be paid overtime wages after a forty-hour work week is a direct result of financial activism by 1930s labor activists, claiming hard-won victory against corporate powers who were quite content working employees out of limbs.[6] (We still have a way to go in ensuring that those at the margins of society, such as migrant workers and incarcerated individuals, are fully included in this win, but the stage has been set to make these advancements possible.)

Today at all levels we owe it to ourselves, the activists before us, and the world that's coming after us, to *choose regeneration*.

Financial Activism Means We Have to Follow the Money

We know that transactions usually follow this logic: *Person A gave person B X dollars in exchange for Y items.* In more nefarious cases, paper trails can offer stories that read more like telenovelas: *Person A gave Person C X dollars (that seems to have magically appeared without record from where . . . sus) to convince Person B to give Y dollars to Person D's business (who just happens to be an in-law of person A).* Even writing that made my head hurt a little. I admire but don't envy financial forensic investigators.

The impacts of financial systems are both tangible and intangible. To one degree or another, finance is playing a role in the sturdiness of the buildings we enter, the quality of the air we breathe, the politicians who hold office, the ability to take bathroom breaks at work, and so on. While money is rarely "real" in the sense of being physical, the effects of the things we assign value to and collectively agree to call money are really, really real.

Beyond exposing eyebrow-raising stories and textbook corruption, paying attention to how and where money moves can be immensely valuable—especially as we imagine carving new grooves for money to flow like water to more people and places. Financial activism invites us to pay attention, track where and how money is currently concentrated in society, and name the increasingly outsized impact that financial systems have on our lives.

Follow the money. Keep your eyes on the ties.

Financial Activism Means We Have to Navigate the Contradictions

Generations of activists and academics are familiar with the proverbial debate teed up by Audre Lorde in 1979—that "the master's tools will never dismantle the master's house."[7] In our case, one might ask: *Why the [BLEEP] would we use tools of finance, if the tools of finance helped get us into this hellhole of inequality?*

As we'll explore together throughout this book, social movements require endless creativity, experimentation, and what activist N'Tanya Lee calls PRINCIPLED STRUGGLE: action for the sake of something larger than ourselves; being honest and direct with each other, while holding compassion.[8] We get to repurpose, modify, and create new tools or strategies that respond to complex, ever-changing conditions—resisting and undoing systems that don't serve us, designing and building ones that do, and always double-checking that we're not reifying a toxic culture in the process.

Sometimes, particularly for those on the political left, debates about revolution versus reform arise (as they should). Where we lose out on opportunities for growth, however, is when we get stuck in heady intellectual conversations and not doing anything at all, leaving money and power just sitting on the table. Our opponents are ready to grab the whole table.

I believe deeply in our agency, but I also know this to be true: under our current capitalist economy and cultural context, *we have no choice but to navigate contradictions.* The material conditions must afford more people the stability to participate in movements and allow them to experience the hope brewed up from tangible wins on the pathway to deeper structural changes. So, sometimes financial activism shows up as an incremental change within an existing system—making something slightly less bad than the convention—and sometimes it shows up as a brand-new innovation, middle fingers blazing to the convention. The simple practice of asking yourself and others if an action is worth doing and the underlying intention of that action, even if it seems tiny, is a move in the right direction.

Setting the Record Straight

In Chapter 3, we'll dive deeper into visioning that right direction and some key elements of the regenerative financial systems that our activism and organizing can help build. But first, let's ground our understanding of what financial activism *is* by also naming what it is *not*.

This section outlines some of the biggest misconceptions and potential pitfalls about this work.

Myth 1: Only Rich People or Elected Government Officials Get to Decide How and Where Money Flows

I detest this unspoken assumption so much that if it were written on a piece of paper, I'd ball it up and shoot it like Steph Curry from the three-point line into a trash can. Then set the trash can on fire.

It's true that some decisions, under the big tent of economic decision-making, require buy-in from those in traditional positions of power, such as bank executives and politicians. But we're focusing here specifically on financial activism *because* it's an effective tool for everyday people, compared to other forms of ECONOMIC ACTIVISM, like MONETARY ACTIVISM (the use of central bank policies, such as interest rate adjustments, to influence a country's money supply and economic conditions) or FISCAL ACTIVISM (involving government actions to manipulate tax and spending policies to stimulate or control a nation's economy).

Financial activism is a tool for everyday people, about the experiences of everyday people.

Myth 2: Financial Activism Means Hating or Loving Money

Money is, in and of itself, a neutral tool. Not a good worth celebrating, nor an evil worth hating.

As social beings we have the funny tendency to animate money, imbuing it with the power to join us in torrid affairs, inducing feelings of stress, intoxication, insatiability, and so on. To be sure, the effects of money *do* often show up as high drama, and understandably so. Drama abounds at all levels. From absence (as in the case of an uninsured medical emergency) to presence (as in the case of budgeting for long-term plans) to abundance (as in the case of a billionaire cheating on his wife and then, in the wake of their divorce, she flexes on him by giving away more in philanthropy than he ever did; yes, I'm talking about MacKenzie Scott—hey girl).[9]

But money alone—think a literal dollar gently floating out of one's palm to the ground—is just a thing. In the same way money can ruin lives, it can be medicine for healing and wholeness when intentionally liberated from a culture of violence and extraction.[10] It can be used as a vehicle for returning what's been stolen, a tool for restoring what's been harmed, and, of course, a kind of alchemy for creating brand-new value and beauty in the world.

Financial activism positions the use of money as a strategic means to an end, or one ingredient in the recipe (albeit a major ingredient . . . like, please don't forget to salt the chicken). For generations, money has been a resource that systems have concentrated into the hands of a few while making it disproportionately challenging to grasp for many others—and it doesn't deserve our passion, one way or another.

Instead, our passion is more useful in fundamentally reimagining the people and systems responsible for how money moves.

Myth 3: Financial Activism = Financial Literacy

Typically, when people say "FINANCIAL LITERACY," they're referring to an individual's knowledge and understanding of financial concepts and personal practices.

I appreciate the people who take to social media platforms and share thirty-second personal finance hacks, like clever ways to increase your savings, how to max out your IRA and get the biggest bang for your buck, or how to diversify by investing in ETFs. For so many content creators, their firsthand experiences—like mounting student debt and housing costs—fuel their desire to democratize access to long-secretive financial knowledge.

So, what's the difference between this kind of work and what we're talking about? To me, financial activism is the cool, more radical cousin of financial literacy. Rather than focus on an individual's money like financial literacy does (*how do I balance my checkbook?*), financial activism zooms out and works to also improve collective financial health (*how do we balance society?*).

"For decades, financial education has been taught from a place of shame, guilt, and judgment, hardly ever considering the systemic issues, past and present, that have made it difficult for minorities to get ahead," shares Dasha Kennedy, founder of @thebrokeblackgirl. "Financial activism bridges the gap between equity and financial education."[11]

Financial activism at its best is an antidote to a financial system that's inaccessible, convoluted, and inequality-producing by design. It's not just about learning how to navigate the system; it's also about changing the system to work for us so that we no longer need to tips-and-tricks our way out of precarious financial situations in the first place.

As this Playbook will continue to remind you, these two concepts of *you* winning and *your community* winning can be one and the same.

Myth 4: Financial Activism Requires Becoming a Financial "Expert"

In my day job being a Big Nerd, I help my team and our clients invest hundreds of millions of dollars into social impact companies and funds. This is true. In my everyday life, I also experience a spike in stress when the bill comes and I pull out my phone to calculate the tip because #mathanxiety.

We contain multitudes.

For some, becoming a finance professional is a walk in the park (and a joyful walk with birds singing and all that, not a scary after-dark walk). For others, me included, our brains don't even particularly like the word *finance*.

That's okay. In fact, people who are financial professionals and experts don't have an inherent learning curve advantage here. That's because their journeys with financial activism often necessitate significant *unlearning* of harmful norms endemic to traditional finance.

As with all movement progress, the most effective efforts and ideas happen because of diverse perspectives coming together. Remember: finance wonks, longtime climate and racial justice advocates, and every-day people just out here living all have a unique role to play in shaping the economy we share.

Myth 5: All We Need Is Financial Activism!

Let me stop you there.

Financial activism can *help* fund storytellers to do the work of changing hearts and minds. It can *support* the ways in which laws are made and policies are adopted. It can *limit* bad actors from screwing over everyday people. Using financial insights and skill sets to reclaim and redistribute resources is critical, but it's by no means the only tool we need to be leveraging in our hefty organizing toolbelt if we want meaningful, lasting change. The role of this Playbook is to help you discern what, when, and how to move money in service of achieving collective goals.

Money is not always the answer. I said what I said.

Myth 6: More Diversity in Our Financial Systems Would Fix Everything

Changing the players without changing the game is a losing strategy. A common false solution that we see branded as "activism" is diversity, equity, and inclusion (DEI) efforts to make our current inequality-producing machines just more "diverse" at the top. Must we remind ourselves that exploitation by women and people of color is still exploitation?

Financial activism *is* about fundamentally challenging a financial system that deems winners take all and the rest can perpetually kick rocks. It's about supporting the emergence of a financial system that allows all of us to truly thrive, given the reality of financial abundance available in the richest period, in the richest nations, in the history of the world. It's about reversing trends of the last fifty years, where $50 trillion in wealth has been stolen from the bottom 90 percent of the population by the top 1 percent of the population, through very explicit financial engineering (more on this coming up).[12]

I promise to refrain from caricaturing billionaires as greedy dragons sitting atop mounds of gold they'll never use, but I won't compromise on the position that having a system that allows anyone to become a billionaire in the first place is more damaging and absurd than it is potentially helpful.[13] Let's imagine that scale of wealth in time. One million minutes is the equivalent of a little less than two years. One billion minutes? One thousand, nine hundred four years. No one needs 1,904 years' worth of minutes. The difference between a billion and a million is bigger than our brains can often comprehend.

The richest 1 percent—who own almost half of the world's wealth—are a natural target for financial activism.[14] That said, we're not here to spend time and energy hating on anyone who's financially flourishing, especially those who a) come from communities where wealth is not guaranteed, and b) made their wealth in non-exploitative ways. Progressive-branded blanket characterizations of just "rich people" as the problem is often

- ◉ a distraction to focus on individual bad actors, rather than on the more powerful underlying problems of bad systems;

- ◉ reinforcing the myth that we must live in a "zero-sum" system, where one person's gain must equal another person's loss;

- ◉ lacking nuance and at odds with the principle of dignity for all; and

- ◉ played out.

So, let's summarize. Romanticizing billionaires without considering where the wealth came from? Not financial activism.

Booing people when they indulge in a nice vacation or spa day while there's still inequality in the world? Weird, and not financial activism.

Using knowledge of financial workings to shift resources into disinvested and historically exploited communities so more people can build wealth and live their most unencumbered lives? Ding ding ding—financial activism!

The system our work aims to shift is the extreme resource concentration that leads to unnecessary, manmade levels of poverty, hunger, and suffering. We could spend the next two hundred pages together laying out different macroeconomic models and philosophical theories, but I'm filing that under "not my job." I also know (sorry, all my very smart academic and pedagogy-disciplined friends and colleagues whom I love so much!) that most people don't really care. They care about sustaining themselves, their families, and their people. They're interested in enjoying life and experiencing a semblance of fairness. *They want to live in a society where everybody eats.*

That's the "radical" economy this Playbook aims to support us ushering in within our lifetimes.

As defined by Angela Davis, "RADICAL simply means grabbing by the root."[15]

CHAPTER 3

The Economy We Deserve, and How We Get There

To put it baldly, there are two ways to become wealthy: to create wealth or to take wealth away from others. The former adds to society. The latter typically subtracts from it, for in the process of taking it away, wealth gets destroyed.

—JOSEPH E. STIGLITZ, *The Price of Inequality*[1]

Let's talk some more about how our dominant economic and financial systems weren't built to last. They just weren't. They're shortsighted by design, rewarding the industries run by individuals who figure out how to make as much money possible as fast as possible, regardless of long-term consequences. They don't operate with the well-being of the vast majority of people and the planet in mind *today*, let alone babies who will be born ten, thirty, fifty years from now.

Speaking of babies and bleakness . . . let's talk about the growing RACIAL WEALTH GAP.[2] Increasingly, white Americans are becoming millionaires by simply *being born* and inheriting generational wealth, making a full one in seven white US families at the time of this writing millionaires, compared to less than two in one hundred Black and Latinx families.[3] I'm not mad at any cute wealthy newborn, but there's nothing cute about a society where financial starting points (based solely on what family you're born into) grow more unequal with each generation.

And let's *finally* as a society talk about . . .

FINANCIALIZATION

. . . the biggest trend most people have never heard of. Financialization is the extractive economy's tactic of engineering financial markets, institutions, and profit motives into virtually every industry, with the goal of shifting wealth away from everyday people and to the BILLIONAIRE CLASS.

ACTION
"Is Our Economy Fair?" Timeline

Take a second to put this book down and open *IsOurEconomyFair.org*, presented by Take on Wall Street, on your phone or computer browser.[4] Spend as much time as you need engaging with the timeline, which will guide you through the key decisions, events, and often forgotten histories of financialization from 1607 to the modern day.

(Spoiler alert regarding the question in the URL: no.)

This is the dirty work of asset managers, HEDGE FUNDS, and other financial entities who influence markets, shape economic policies, and have turned the finance industry into a larger and larger part of global economies—growing economic metrics like GDP without growing real well-being for everyday people. (Pay attention to the "Big Three" players—Blackrock, Vanguard, and State Street—ASSET MANAGEMENT COMPANIES that have ownership in virtually all major corporations on the planet.)

"The 1 percent don't 'create wealth,'" writes author Marjorie Kelly in her book *Wealth Supremacy*, "they extract it . . . from the pockets of ordinary people, our common government, and the planet."[5] It's why, adjusting for inflation, the average American worker's wages have mostly stayed the same for fifty years, while average CEO pay has sky-rocketed by more than 1,460 percent.[6]

"In the past few decades, the American economy generated lots of income and wealth that would have allowed substantial living standards gains for every family," explains the Economic Policy Institute (EPI). But that hasn't happened, by design.[7]

As financial activists, the challenge in front of us as outlined by the EPI is whether we redesign systems to "enable everyone to participate in a shared prosperity," or whether "the growth of income and wealth will continue to accrue excessively and disproportionately to the best-off 1 percent."[8]

Reversing financialization is part of how we collectively transition away from an extractive economy and financial culture, and toward building a regenerative one. Wealth must be redefined not by how much someone takes and stockpiles, but by the value they share and spread. And how we actually go about that transition from extractive to regenerative can be grounded in deeply intentional practices, principles, and processes that *build power*—known widely in climate and social movement spaces as a *Just Transition*.[9]

Moving Away from Extraction, Toward Regeneration, with a Just Transition

The JUST TRANSITION framework and culturally relevant analogues are already being used in practice by communities around the world. The framework, illustrated in Figure 3.1, was first developed by the trade union movement and then built upon by organizers from environmental and climate justice communities like Movement Generation and Climate Justice Alliance.

The framework makes clear that no community or ecosystem is expendable in a regenerative economy. For example, as we work to diminish the role of fossil fuels, do dying coal miner communities have access to training and better jobs in the clean energy sector? Are veterans of our distant wars truly supported to integrate back into peaceful society? Have we built sufficiently affordable neighborhood grocery alternatives to Walmart and Amazon Prime?

a just transition looks like...

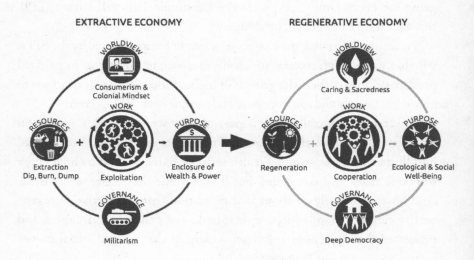

FIGURE 3.1. Just Transition Framework (used with permission from Climate Justice Alliance and Movement Generation)

ACTION
From Banks and Tanks to Cooperation and Caring

For the visually minded, I also highly recommend opening up the web page *MovementGeneration.org/JustTransition/* and downloading the beautiful zine *From Banks and Tanks to Cooperation and Caring*.

In addition to the digital version, you can also order hard copies of the zine in bulk for your community or organization. Trust me, they're great to gift (and use as coloring books).

Hold Up: How Do We Decide What to Prioritize?

There's a lot to be done. What's more, movement demands tend to be iterative and dynamic responses to on-the-ground conditions, rather than stagnant and linear goals.

As we navigate financial activist strategies, our brains are at some point likely to face a "paradox of choice."[10] Simply put, too many options can induce stress and make us feel less confident about our ultimate decisions, sometimes to the point of total inaction. The menus of both possible problems and possible ways to address said problems are, quite literally, endless.

So, we have a few ways to approach this paradox of choice in decision-making at any given time:

1. Do, um, nothing. Common, but safe to say not what you're here for.

2. Do something based on your best judgment. Closer, but not without limitations.

3. Do something based on your best judgment, which is informed by and in real SOLIDARITY with the minds and spirits who make up the fabric of our progressive social movements.

This Playbook calls for choosing option 3 wherever the opportunity presents itself.

Many of us—especially my fellow overthinkers and the generally overwhelmed—can find deep relief in knowing that diverse coalitions of countless grassroots activists, organizers, researchers, and creatives *have already done the work* of identifying both big problems and big solutions through decades of organizing partnerships.

PEOPLE POWER is what happens when we mesh all that beautiful expertise together and observe and tend to the trends that serve the most expansive definition of "us."

I've found myself cringing in the impact investing and philanthropic field when those with a lot of financial capital interested in doing good are encouraged to choose a single issue or two that "most resonates" with them (Women's rights! The environment! Closing the racial wealth gap!), as if all social and climate issues aren't inherently connected. What makes this reductionist strategy dangerous is that money is then allocated in themed ways—neglecting to consider potential unintended consequences to those outside that focus and passing up opportunities for even deeper intersectional impact. This could show up as investments into solar-powered killing machines or eco-friendly products manufactured under unethical working conditions.

In this new age of financial activism, we can and should follow the leads of those most intimately impacted by the messy, intersecting, pressing social issues of this moment (and all the moments to come). We can resource social change—not based on the whims of one particularly wealthy family's potentially fleeting passion, but by following the road maps designed in deep movement integrity. We can respond to existing, clearly articulated calls to action, instead of putting the burden on ourselves to sort through the impossibly cacophonous noise of needs. And we can humble ourselves by knowing that *not everything is our job to do.*

Principles to Lean On

Small individual actions that are in alignment with and intentional about common goals add up to big movements. This section offers some principles to help you stay aligned and intentional.

1. Center the Margins

We're working toward a next economy where everyone's needs are met and sustained, with dignity. This requires deep collaboration across very different experiences—recognizing the common financial forces at play behind issues like the gentrification of historically Black inner cities, the opioid crisis in rural white America, resource exploitation on Native lands, and financial colonization across the whole world.

The most strategic way to make sure no one is left behind in redesign is by following leadership from "THE MARGINS": those who are most overlooked or intentionally exploited by current power structures. A clear example of this happened in the summer of 2019, when activists from East Michigan Environmental Council, Climate Justice Alliance,

It Takes Roots, and People's Action were joined by sixty-four front-line and allied organizations in Detroit to participate in the "Frontline Green New Deal + Climate and Regenerative Economy Summit." Out of that convening came the foundational resource *A People's Orientation to a Regenerative Economy*, which does the important work of taking existing popular progressive policy proposals and further specifying *who* we need to invest in, and how.[11]

ACTION
Explore Priorities for and by Everyday People

Collective agenda setting is, of course, easier said than done. There isn't a way to SparkNotes social movements and organizing: understanding their full sophistication and vibrancy takes time, commitment, and direct participation. However, there are valuable resources that detail digestible, curated demands and that have the brainpower and backing of countless individuals from historically impacted identities across the globe.

Search for and open *A People's Orientation to a Regenerative Economy* on your internet-enabled device and read through the fourteen "planks." *Notice which planks you're most familiar with, and which you haven't given much thought to yet.*

_____

_____

A People's Orientation gives us an example of actively centering those at the margins of society by listening to the wisdom of people who experience multiple dimensions of societal marginalization simultaneously, such as racism and sexism, or ableism and homophobia. This prioritization is key for addressing the root causes rather than just the nasty symptoms of financial injustice.

2. Prioritize Democratic Systems

As defined by New Economy Coalition, a *solidarity economy* is an ecosystem where all the things a community needs are controlled and governed by everyday people: housing, schools, farms and food production, local governance structures, art and culture, healthcare and healing, and transportation.[12] This transformation requires an embracing of our interconnectedness, and the reality that not having a solid community to lean on (and have lean back) is bad for our health.

Yes, it's human nature to have conflict, but it's also human nature to be cooperative and sustain our communities for generations. We're biologically motivated to pass along DNA, but we're also wired to strive for fulfillment and connection and belonging, not just survival. Let's take some time to sit with and appreciate our beautiful complexities and how they complement each other.

Systems and practices like the SOLIDARITY ECONOMY that value equality, participation, and representation of the people may not always be easy ... but they're worth it. When assessing opportunities for financial activism, we can choose targets that bring us closer to the promise of real democracy.

3. Remember We Have Great Teachers in Nature

I've learned from impact investor Deborah Frieze that nature may serve as a better model than markets for financial activists.

For example, our economic cultures often prioritize hogweed finance over hardwood forest finance. Stay with me.

A hardwood tree takes over ten years to reach maturity, which means it could take over a decade for seedlings in a forest to truly become, well, a forest and not just a bunch of individual trees. Slow, steady, sturdy—or, as the late great rapper and community investor Nipsey Hussle would call it, a marathon. Once those trees are locked in, there's a whole magical underground world (i.e., root systems and fungal networks) through which the trees communicate, pass along resources, and sustain one another for hundreds of years.

Compare that to a more invasive, colonizing species like hogweed, whose stalk can grow more than a foot tall *per day*, chaotically destroying and taking over all the plant life around it in the process. Not a fun species to hang around!

BIOMIMICRY is like a cheat sheet for human flourishing and economics that Indigenous peoples have leaned on for millennia: it's the understanding that there's endless wisdom to glean from nature in creating, maintaining, and sustaining systems.[13]

The largest hardwood tree could hypothetically hoard all the sunlight and nutrients, but it instead redistributes those essential goodies as a part of ensuring that the entire forest thrives. We also know that our tall and generous friend is never going to give away *all* its nutrients and sacrifice itself. The hardwood tree has no ego that says, "I'm gonna take one for the team, bye!" and then just wilts away in hopes that the forest is better off without it.

In our movements, too often we see individuals burn out because of overgiving and forgetting to tend to their own needs. Nature has a humbling lesson for us.

"The trees act not as individuals, but somehow as a collective," writes Potawatomi botanist Robin Wall Kimmerer.[14] "What happens to one happens to us all. We can starve together or feast together."

Nature teaches us that a sensible economy is like a forest built to last, in which we never forget that each of us belongs.

4. Don't Aim for "Perfect" (or Get Tripped Up by Colonial Thinking)

Perfection is the enemy of progress. It's also an unrealistic—yet normalized—cultural standard in our dominant financial system, weaponized by colonialist and imperial projects across time and space. So maybe we stay away from perfectionism in our financial activism, okay?

Stewarded by artist, activist, and academic Tema Okun, the website *WhiteSupremacyCulture.info* hosts a handy curated list of "characteristics of WHITE SUPREMACY CULTURE" that we're so deeply steeped in, they often go unnoticed.[15]

The list includes the following:

- One right way/perfectionism
- Fear
- Either/or and the binary
- Denial and defensiveness
- Right to comfort and fear of conflict
- Individualism
- Progress is "more" and quantity over quality
- Worship of the written word
- Urgency

EXERCISE
No, Thank You, White Supremacy Culture

Take a second to reflect:

- How and where does our current relationship to finance reinforce these characteristics?

- What characteristics might we replace these tendencies with, as we collectively build out a healthier economy and culture?

The next time one of these characteristics shows up in your everyday experience, and you find yourself thinking, *Hmm, I wonder if this is white supremacy culture showing up*, just say, "No, thank you." To yourself. Or out loud.

---

5. Embrace Nuance and Emergence

We're each positioned to bring unique resources and attributes to build the next economy. Inspired by writer adrienne marie brown's book *Emergent Strategy*, successful financial activism entails properties and behaviors that emerge only when the parts interact in a wider whole.[16]

It may be hard to conceptualize EMERGENCE or recognize when it's happening, but you've likely tasted it. The best meals (curries, stews, paellas, you name it) aren't just a matter of individual ingredients coming together. They're the surprising new flavors that emerge when ingredients work in symphony, the wisdom passed along from one generation to the next, the techniques and creative endeavors based on what's available, and the recipes that are modified and remixed based on trial and ~~error~~ eating.

In other words, our contributions are so much more than the sum of our parts.

I'm continuously inspired by people who hold multiple truths about these times: that emerging from the global COVID-19 pandemic is a moment of haunting losses, energetic opportunity, and joyful reprioritization. The pandemic illuminated existing system failures and humbling disruptions, and, to a degree, socialized the masses to concepts of vast change and adaptation. As we increasingly understand the fragility and interconnectivity of our economy, we can grieve the people, businesses, and norms no longer with us while honoring radical inclusion in our rebuilding (and reimagining) processes. We get to weed out what no longer serves us, plant new seeds, tend to what's emerging, and revel in new blooms.

This Playbook, by virtue of its format, outlines a finite number of strategies. Eight, to be exact. However, multiplied by the creativity of readers (and iconized by the genius of the 2004 film *Mean Girls*), we know that the limit does not exist. Again, the whole is greater than the sum of its parts.

Alongside changing our relationships to money, financial activism reminds us to take stock of now, imagine tomorrow, and embrace the unexpected. The ways in which we can contribute and flow money will always be dynamic, whether we're talking about periods of mass dumpster-fire chaos or seemingly mundane and stable times. Even if you picked up this Playbook without any idea about how you'd use its tools, I hope you find excitement in knowing you've accepted the invitation to be part of the mass reclamation of our wealth.

You now know what financial activism is. Ready to dive into the strategies?

PART II
THE STRATEGIES

These eight core strategies of financial activism are ours to experiment with.

CHAPTER 4

Strategy 1,
Talking about Money

If we're all so "bad with money," maybe the problem isn't us. Maybe it's the confusing and inaccessible ways how money and power are organized . . . we can't dismantle [the system], work to fix what's broken, or engage politically if we can't begin to understand it.

—GABE DUNN, *Bad with Money*[1]

In an **extractive** financial system, talking about money is often "taboo," lacking transparency, individualistic, and straight up confusing.

In a **regenerative** financial system, talking about money is normalized, open, community-centric, and accessible for all.

By reclaiming how and why we talk about money, we become equipped to spot and challenge financial exploitation, get clear about our personal and collective goals, and empower others to craft a fairer economy.

P olitics. Death. Existential crises.
   Waiting in the DMV line. Having the ending to a TV show spoiled. Missing a flight.
   These are some of the topics of conversation and experiences that people prefer over discussing their finances, according to a 2023 survey

of two thousand US adults.[2] Over six in ten people admit to not talking about money at all, and one in four recalls being taught as a child that bringing it up is "impolite."

In a society where we know money talks, the average person is pretty used to staying quiet about the proverbial elephant in the room.

Near the end of her father's life, Nafasi Ferrell recalls going with him to Chase Bank to sign some paperwork and be designated as his beneficiary.[3] "He said, 'You know, you got it. You'll figure it out.' [I'm like] . . . what are we figuring out?" she recalls with a laugh.

His passing in 2018 was a shock to her nervous system, and picking up the pieces revealed new layers of his life that Nafasi realized she knew very little about. In her brother's basement, she sifted through piles of her dad's things and came across a pretty, shiny piece of paper. "[I thought] it must be . . . I don't know, some propaganda or something. So, I ripped it up."

The pretty, shiny piece of paper turned out to be her father's stock papers.

"[No one told] me what stock was, or how stock worked, or that he even had any stock!" she reflects. Nafasi had to pay a frustrating fee to reclaim the assets, but the moment paid her back in more ways than one. She began to question out loud: Why don't we talk about our finances? And what would happen if we did?

Nafasi's journey of curiosity to understand her finances was fueled by free YouTube videos and countless conversations with others getting real about the role of money in their lives. This bravery to take agency over financial matters would ultimately help her get herself and her husband out of $30,000 of consumer debt.

We don't know what we don't know. This is where the power of community comes in. Today, through her company, Narratives Unbound, Nafasi is dedicated to helping others not only pay down their lurking debt and redistribute wealth, but also reclaim the powerful right to talk about finances collectively.[4]

While it may be tempting to pooh-pooh the role of PERSONAL FINANCE in the much larger work of COLLECTIVE LIBERATION, talking about money as a new cultural practice can be a powerful spell to cast on forces like pay inequity and financial gatekeeping. Indeed, encouraging research shows that millennials and Gen Z are less guarded when it comes to money topics compared to older generations, and are twice as likely to say they're an "open book."[5] Bravery has a ripple effect, and the work of reframing our finances as numbers, not knives, takes more than just "financial literacy." It takes conversation.

The Trauma of Money

Chantel Chapman, a high school graduate, served the same group of men every Friday at the Vancouver, Canada, restaurant where she waitressed.[6] The type of men one might call "successful," "big ballers," or "put together." One day she asked them what they do for a living.

"We're mortgage brokers!" they shared. She asked how they got into that, and the men said something to the effect of, "Well, it's really easy, actually. You take a course, wait a few months . . . no prerequisites needed." So, Chantel took the course and became a mortgage broker (no prerequisites needed) and started a career helping potential homebuyers secure loans from lending institutions.

The only problem was, those potential homebuyers weren't keen to take seriously someone who, at twenty-one years old, looked like she might still live with her parents. As a result, Chantel wasn't landing a ton of clients. Or rather, she was, but only the ones who had already been declined by banks for home loans because of their financial histories and low credit scores.

In getting to know her pushed-to-the-sidelines clients, she couldn't understand why banks continued to deny them loans even when they had the money to pay. These were people who had been working hard for years to garner stability for themselves and their families. They were good people. And she gets pissed off when good people get treated badly.

"I felt really angry because I was in a similar situation. I had lots of credit card debt, I was underearning. . . . And so I really believed, you know—if they *only* taught financial literacy in high school, [we] wouldn't have any of these problems."

Fixing the Canadian public education curriculum to include financial literacy classes is a big task for one person, but Chantel did something else pretty significant: she opened up her own financial literacy advocacy business. She was all in, unearthing the shady secrets of how credit scores were calculated, helping everyday people repair their financial health, and consulting big corporations to do better and make education accessible. She even helped develop Canada's first-ever free credit score program.

You read that right: an incredible feat of financial activism! Without a college degree, Chantel identified a big problem—the fact that people who wanted to improve their credit scores couldn't *check* their credit scores without being penalized—and then advocated for a tangible solution to help make the system more equitable. Not to mention she built her passion into a career and helped a lot of people repair their credit! Go, Chantel!

. . . but this story doesn't end there. Her success had a funny taste to it.

"[I] was consulting at this executive level. I'm supposed to be this 'expert' around money, [but I was still in] credit card debt, overspending, undercharging, [experiencing] workaholism. . . ." She started seeing different therapists and was diagnosed with complex PTSD and obsessive-compulsive disorder.

So now let's go back to the real beginning: before she began waitressing and meeting the fancy mortgage broker guys. Chantel shares a photo of herself as a smiling, blonde-haired, bright-eyed baby, sitting on the lap of two stunning women in front of a Sears photo studio backdrop: blue eye shadow, big hair, the whole 1980s glam. "This is my mom and my mom's best friend. Her best friend had just turned twenty in this photo. In my early years, I was raised by these two lovely women." Despite the wealth of love that's so evident in this picture, Chantel lived in poverty.

"I grew up in an environment that was very chaotic," she says. Her mom was always working and stressed about money. Her brother's dad came into the picture when she was about four, along with his heroin addiction and abusive tendencies. She witnessed, and experienced, years of sexual, physical, and emotional abuse in the home. "I developed a very, very strong narrative around money, and that was . . . if we had more money, I would have been safe. Those bad things wouldn't happen to me."

In a move not unlike the admirable go-getter patterns we now know are characteristic of Chantel, she put her more-money-equals-less-chaos equation to the test. Specifically, by choosing serious romantic relationships with men who possessed extreme wealth. When she was seventeen, that wealthy partner also happened to be heavily involved in organized crime.

"I lived in a home where we had bars on our windows, and my nervous system felt safe in that, even though rationally and logically, I was not safe because the risk of a drive-by shooting was significant." Fortunately, she was able to get out of the relationship, escaping violence that three years later would put her ex on the cover of a local newspaper after suffering a gunshot wound due to his gang involvement.

When she began making decent money for herself as an adult, she was painfully reminded again that you need a lot more than excess cash and financial literacy to heal old wounds. A close contact called her asking for help: they admitted they were addicted to fentanyl. "I threw myself into their recovery like a good codependent does . . . there I was, at that [halfway] house. Every day I was bringing [the people in recovery] food. I was meditating with them, and doing everything I could to support their recovery." In her conversations with this person, trying to understand why someone so close to her ended up in this battle with addiction, Chantel realized they weren't the only ones with unhealthy patterns stemming from a sense of unworthiness and a desire to numb the pain.

"I just kind of thought about all of my [financial] behaviors, the people pleasing. . . . Wow, those things are my substances, but society encourages me to do them." And then it hit her. "I'm like, 'Oh, my gosh'—the anger I had about the lack of financial literacy . . . that anger is misdirected. It's trauma.

[My relationship with money] . . . it's trauma."

Cue the start of a new chapter for our beloved financial activist: developing the Trauma of Money method.[7]

Decreasing Shame, Increasing Discernment

1. Question "Why is this like this?"

Show me a person living under modern capitalism, and I'll show you someone who has experienced money trauma. If that sounds like hyperbole, let's consider what I mean when I use words like TRAUMA.

Broadly speaking, *trauma* is a distressing event, set of patterns, or inherited history that threatens *someone's sense of physical safety and/or sense of identity*. "FINANCIAL TRAUMA [is] an emotional wounding that happens as a direct result of something to do specifically with money," Chantel explains.[8] In ways both subtle and direct, many of us are raised in a culture where we're taught that how much money we have is the direct outcome only of how hard we work, and in turn, how "deserving" and "worthy" we are as individuals.

We often think about big T Traumas (singular major accidents, significant losses, episodes of violence) without attending to little t traumas (inheriting debt, experiencing food insecurity, consistently being bullied about money).[9] And then there's collective trauma (cue mass insecurity in the wake of bank failures and global pandemics), ancestral trauma (from the generational violence of colonization to the fact that, a few generations ago, our grandmas couldn't open bank accounts in their name), which all accumulate in our relationships with money.

In 2019, Chantel began partnering with trauma-informed practitioners from a breadth of marginalized identities to launch The Trauma of Money, or TOM (*TheTraumaOfMoney.com*), as a seventeen-week online course for professionals like therapists and financial advisors, as well as everyday people, who are interested in diving deep into healing money traumas and creating financial well-being. The goal is to help people increase discernment and decrease shame on their individual and organizational financial journeys.

When we're operating from places of shame, fear, and real or assumed scarcity, as the TOM framework suggests, we're making decisions from a place of survival, rather than cognitively. In other words, the decisions we make are reactions instead of actions. Those reactions can and do reverberate to those around us.

So, how do we begin rebuilding better, less traumatizing financial systems? First, we start by reclaiming our individual nervous systems and narratives around money so that we're well positioned to act
collaboratively.

"If we want to show up in transformative collective change work,
and we show up from a place of scarcity, or we show up from a place of
an activated trauma state, it really impacts our ability to collaborate and
to co-create," Chantel reminds us. "Taking individual responsibility for
your own nervous system actually contributes to the collective healing
of everyone else."

It's time to get personal, beloved reader.

From Money Scripts to Money Stories

In interviewing mental health professionals for this book, I heard
repeatedly that talking about money was never something that came up
in formal training, leaving them feeling unequipped when they began to
practice and found the *majority* of their clients' major stresses could be
linked to money in some way. Fortunately, the tides are changing, and
the field of psychology is taking the effects of financial stress seriously.

Dr. Brad Klontz is the co-founder of the Financial Psychology Institute, focusing on the intersection of personal finance and behavioral
psychology.[10] He and his colleagues offer four *money scripts*—archetypes
of unconscious beliefs and attitudes that shape financial decision-
making—that most people fall into, shaped by collective experiences
and systems (see Figure 4.1):

- **Money avoidance.** *Money is the root of all evil.* People with this
  script may experience guilt about the money they do have, avoid
  dealing with financial matters altogether, or associate pursuing
  money with compromising their values. In other words, they
  believe more money, more problems.

- **Money worship.** *Money is the key to happiness.* People with this script
  may prioritize wealth accumulation over everything, take big risks
  in pursuit of big returns, or have compulsive spending tendencies.
  In other words, they believe more money, more freedom.

- **Money vigilance.** *Money is meant to be saved.* People with this script are always budgeting, are hesitant to spend or take financial risks, or generally have a hard time enjoying the presence of money. In other words, they believe more money, more anxiety.

- **Money status.** *Money is meant to be endlessly multiplied.* People with this script may feel a constant need to "prove" their wealth, seek validation from others through material possessions, or care a lot about social comparisons. In other words, they believe more money, more self-worth.

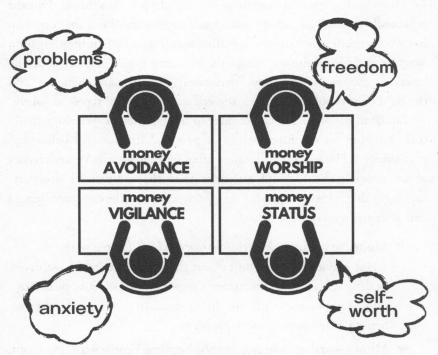

FIGURE 4.1. The four money scripts (adapted from Dr. Brad Klontz)

Now, you may have immediately pointed at one of these scripts and said, "Uh oh, that's me," but it's important to note some nuance. First, an individual may hold a combination of **MONEY SCRIPTS**, and may lean more heavily on one script or another at different points in their life. Second, please remember this is a certified No Judgment Zone. No money script is "better" or "worse" than another, and each can feed healthy or unhealthy behaviors. This offering of the four money scripts is a useful *starting place* to inquire and gain insights about your relationship to money to make more conscious, informed, and compassionate decisions moving forward.

ACTION
Money Script Inventory

2. Check-in "How do I feel about this?"

If you like, you can pause reading to search and *take the Klontz Money Script® Inventory-Revised (KMSI-R) test* from your internet-enabled device of choice.[11] Feel free to write out what you learn in the margins and to what degree you agree or disagree with the assessment.

Ready to get even more personal? Unlike money scripts, *money stories* are as unique to each person as fingerprints, even if two people come from the same class, culture, or household. We know stories matter: they're the precious currency passed from one generation to the next, memorialized through art, and responsible for shaping worldviews.

There's wealth in the story of you and yours.

If you're ready to start thinking through, speaking about, or writing out your **MONEY STORY** in full—whether that's in a voice note to yourself or in a letter draft you might like to share one day—the following sections offer some prompts to respond to.

ANCESTRAL STORY

⊙ Who are your people? Where did they call home(s)?

⊙ What do you (or don't you) know about the role of financial systems in their lives?

⊙ What financial wealth did they have (property, savings, gold jewelry, etc.)?

⊙ What nonfinancial wealth did they have (community ties, skill sets, knowledge, etc.)?

There may be gaps, unknowns, and guesses as you read these questions, especially if your family story includes slavery, migration, and dispossession. There may also be grief, remembrance, and inspiration. Take time to honor the ancestors that got you here—call a family member, imagine what brought your great-great granny joy, or do whatever practice feels right and available to you at this moment.

As Indigenous wisdom reminds us: in the past seven generations, it took 128 grandparents to bring you into this world. I'm grateful to each of them for the very fact you're here reading.

GROWING UP STORY

⊙ How was money talked about or handled in your family or community?

⊙ How might early experiences and lessons in your upbringing have shaped your views on the financial system?

⊙ Reflect on standout financial events or milestones in your life: getting your first job, taking on debt, receiving an inheritance, or achieving a financial goal. How did these events impact your financial well-being and how you think and feel about money?

ACTION:
Class Privilege Quiz

Resource Generation organizes the richest 10 percent of progressive eighteen-to-thirty-five-year-olds in the US who have access to wealth and class privilege, providing a community of practice to facilitate their equitable distribution of wealth, land, and power.[12] Even if you already know you're not in the highest income bracket, their online **CLASS PRIVILEGE QUIZ** offers a valuable starting place for assessing where you land, with wide-ranging prompts like "You have a safety net from friends and/or family to fall back on if needed," "You've never had an issue affording healthcare and regular doctor's visits," "You've been on a yacht," and "Heck, you OWN a yacht."

Take a pause here; open the quiz on your laptop, phone, tablet, smartwatch, or other device; and write down the results here for reference.

CURRENT STORY

- How do you generally flow money *into* your life?
- How do you generally flow money *out* of your life?
- How much money do you have?*

EXERCISE
Net Wealth Exploration

*The question "How much money do you have?" seems like it should be straightforward, but research shows most of us have little to no idea about the number tied to our net worth. That's okay. The concept of net worth is oversimplified and, frankly, ridiculous. Your "worth" is in no way defined by your financial assets, okay? Okay.

Still, understanding and tracking our net ~~worth~~ wealth can be a helpful tool for right-sizing our financial decisions and the risks we can take on. The equation for this is:

Net Wealth = Assets – Liabilities

1. To calculate your financial assets, make a list and add up the amounts of any:

   - Cash
   - Bank account balances
   - Retirement accounts (401(k), IRA, pension plans)
   - Investments (stocks, bonds, mutual funds, etc.)
   - Real estate properties you own (primary residence, rental properties, land)
   - Vehicles (cars, motorcycles, boats, etc.)
   - Business interests or ownership
   - Other valuable possessions (jewelry, artwork, collectibles)

2. To calculate your financial liabilities, make a list and add up the amounts of any:

   - Credit card debt
   - Student loans
   - Mortgage/real estate loans
   - Auto loans
   - Personal loans
   - Other outstanding debts

3. Subtract the second number from the first number, and voilà! A snapshot of your current financial net wealth.

It may take some time to wrangle these numbers, *but setting aside an hour or so every few months (or even once a quarter) can be good hygiene for your financial health.* I ritualize this practice by setting a time to FaceTime my dad (my personal finance cheerleader), getting out my favorite notebook (adorned with an Intelligent Mischief sticker that reads "What if we had the autonomy to choose what comes next?"), and walking through each step out loud.

FUTURE STORY

3. Map "What's possible?"

- What will more equitable financial systems enable for collective well-being in five years? Ten years? Thirty years?
- What types of financial assets and investments will be important to you and your community?
- What do you dream your descendants will remember about your contributions to the world?

Sample Money Stories

Money stories can be a few sentences or entire memoirs long. Here's a brief family money story my friend Esther Park shared:[13]

> My parents saw an opportunity to come to the United States and get higher education and to seek out a better life. . . . They just came here with nothing but the clothes on their backs, and maybe a little bit of money. My dad got a job with the State of California, so they moved up to Sacramento and they established themselves there.
>
> [Also,] they were entrepreneurs . . . they were successful with business, and they were able to put their kids through high

school, college, all of that, and lead out a pretty middle-class life. Just your typical immigrant, "pull yourself up by your boot-straps" kind of story.

Here's a second money story:

Both of my parents were the second youngest of seven children in each of their families. My mother had [an] older brother, who came to the United States before she did. He had already established himself and established a family, and so when she came to the United States, she was able to live with him and his family for a little while before she got settled in school. They very much helped her settle in, they helped her get acclimated to the new context and culture of the United States.

My dad also had a brother who already lived in St. Louis, so he ended up going to the University of Missouri so he could be near his brother. And again, his brother helped him get established while he was going to school. So then, when my dad came out to California and met my mom, [and] when they started to think about opening a business of their own, they opened a dry-cleaning business.

. . . because my mom already had a sister and brother here in the States who had opened dry-cleaning businesses. Because there was a Korean community here in California that had sort of figured out how to do these dry-cleaning businesses. [M]y uncle learned how to do it. He taught my aunt how to do it, and then he taught my parents how to do it, and so they were able to establish this business because of their relatives and generate some additional income to get their family to a middle-income kind of situation.

4. Ask yourself "What can I do right now?"

The above are both Esther's stories. The first framing leans more into the individualized narrative that you can make something out of nothing if you just work hard and try your best. The second, more detailed story is one of community economics—of housing, of investment in one another's stability, of unlocking additional income for one another.

There is no one whose money story is the result of their decisions and actions alone. How we talk about money, people, and systems matters.

As you share your money story with others, I invite you to lean into the truth telling that only you have the power to do, especially when it comes to naming investments that others made in you, in any form.

Now, we know there's power in looking your finances in the face. What might be possible if we demanded that organizations and institutions be more transparent about money, too?

Transparency, Together

My first job offer after college was at a fancy Manhattan consulting firm, run by a powerful, cartoonishly rich woman CEO who promised to be my mentor and give me an "out of the ballpark," "unheard of" starting salary that would change my financial position. I couldn't believe my luck.

I hadn't even applied for a job—just spent some time as an unpaid intern organizing spreadsheets. It was a far cry from the nonprofit positions I had been eyeing, and though I didn't 100 percent understand what the firm *did* (first red flag), I knew it involved supporting the reputations of very important clients who had millions and even billions of dollars to their names. It was a self-described "feminist organization" that was working to "empower women to make the world a better place," and my deep research experience and knowledge of social movements were positioned as a unique asset to the firm. I had all but signed my name on a dotted line.

And then I asked for more details. Graduation was approaching, and I was eager to learn just how much this "unheard of" starting salary would be. Over the phone, my mentor and soon-to-be boss said a lot of things I didn't fully understand like "W-9" and "NDAs," and when I finally caught a number in her words, my heart sank. The salary offer was less than I was making hourly as a lifeguard.

What happened next was not so fun at the time but makes me smile in retrospect. I called my parents with the news that I'd been offered this salary and their immediate response was laughter, followed by anger and many expletives, followed by "Absolutely not. Call her back." Shaking, I scheduled another call with this CEO—my trusted mentor! Who for months had, for some reason, been taking time out of her wealthy boss lady life to court me!—and clumsily asked something like "Well, um, you told me to advocate for myself as a woman, so, respectfully, is it possible for me to negotiate on the salary?"

She told me to never speak to her again and hung up the phone.

This moment, friends, was filled with so much embarrassment. I was sure I fumbled the bag and should have just accepted the role (and that I had zero other prospects and would never, ever get a job).

It turns out that rejection was beyond a blessing. Years later, I was informed that this wealthy white woman CEO had demonstrated a long pattern of hiring—wanna guess?—all young women of color and immigrants as her staff, whom she would underpay and emotionally abuse, leading to a discrimination lawsuit against her. And that top-secret reputation work for high-powered clients? To my understanding, we're talking everything from damage control for male executives who were embroiled in the #MeToo movement for sexual harassment to universities who wanted insights on how to quell student activism on campus. To top it all off: the firm was able to erase negative online comments about employee experiences.

I spent years being silent about this experience, first ashamed that I almost fell into the trap, then ashamed that I did nothing to make sure other young women didn't go through the same. But now I'm grateful for the experience and what it taught me: without trusted others to be a sounding board, financial exploitation is a lot harder to spot and fend off.

When we each choose to break taboos around money conversations, we challenge harmful cultures that thrive on secrecy and undervaluing people. Increasingly, activists are winning collective policy victories that hold employers accountable to pay transparency, such as requiring companies to share the pay range for positions up front, and not being able to retaliate against employees who discuss their wages with other employees.

5. Ask your community "What can we do together?"

And talking about money isn't only liberatory for fighting exploitation. It can also lead to ease and aha moments with those closest to you in ways that make even the most boring bits of finance fun. Author of *Money Out Loud* and professional financial hype woman Berna Anat describes her financial activism as "yanking back the shame and powerlessness" so many of us feel around money.[14] One of her favorite ways to do this? Throwing a Tax Brunch.

"I invited all my fellow money-anxious friends to my apartment, provided snax and dranx, and we all whipped out our laptops and searched for legit tax resources and/or screamed our confusion together." Yup. Even handling taxes together can be empowering.

The Future Is Vocal

Let's recap a few of the ways that talking about money can build relationships and power:

- ⊙ **Exchange money stories.** When we choose to share our money stories, we create opportunities to see and be seen, discover our own biases and assumptions, and feel less alone in the messy experience of extractive capitalism.

- ⊙ **Demystify fair pay and prices**. From realizing employers may be skimping on overtime pay to deciding whether the interest rate on a loan is fair, community can provide a treasure trove of financial data points.

- ⊙ **Reclaim joy and safety around money to-dos**. How subversive is it to take something as dreadful as filing taxes or paying down debt and instead make it a ritual with loved ones you actually look forward to?

For many of us, discussion of the financial system evokes confusion, frustration, anxiety, and, in the *best-case* scenario, straight-up boredom. The reason the complex world of finance feels intentionally exclusionary and mysterious is because, well, it is. It's intimidating by design. But jargon aside, many concepts within finance can be straightforward. By choosing to have transparent, trauma-informed, curious conversations about our relationships to finance, we become pattern-breakers unlocking new possibilities.

Let's keep the conversation going, unapologetically.

CHAPTER 5

Strategy 2,
Banking on Ourselves

*The wellbeing of a community and the economic
health of its banks are usually correlated.*

—MEHRSA BARADARAN, *The Color of Money*[1]

In an **extractive** financial system, banking institutions have normalized short-term profit maximization, predatory lending practices, funding social and environmental devastation, and exploitation of bank customers and communities.

In a **regenerative** financial system, banking looks like long-term sustainable investments, ethical and inclusive lending practices, funding social and environmental thriving, and empowerment of bank customers and communities.

By reclaiming how and why we bank, we can help our savings grow and flow toward building a fairer economy.

"They were like, 'Okay, make sure you wear some reliable shoes,'" laughs thirty-nine-year-old Stephone Coward II, recounting the confusion of nineteen-year-old Stephone Coward II on the phone with his new employer.[2]

Back home for his first summer break from the University of Texas at Arlington, and more than ready to make some money, he headed to the local hardware-store-slash-lumberyard for his first day on the job as a cashier. Except when he arrived, he most definitely wasn't placed behind the cashier in the air-conditioned store, but instead out in the "slash-lumberyard" part of the equation, loading doors and windows into trucks in the heat. "I swear it was the hottest summer ever and it was like two weeks of doing that until I was like, 'Nah. Can't do it. Not me.'"

His next summer employment attempt landed him in the cool back office of another seemingly straightforward local institution: a bank outside the military community where he lived. With the world's friendliest face and a love for talking to people, Stephone moved from the back office to bank teller, where he excelled at helping community members open accounts and process transactions. That's the industry he stayed in for close to two decades—finishing school, working, supporting himself, and applying to jobs at a new bank when the bank he was working at shut down.

And shut down it did. On his daily drives to work, Stephone noticed fewer banks and more payday loan centers filling shopping centers. Every other commercial on the radio would be "Do you need $1,000 now?" with a cute little jingle. When he asked community leaders for answers on disappearing banks, he got versions of "Well, the bank people deemed that the communities weren't profitable."

Ah, now we're getting somewhere.

The communities were predominantly Black and brown North Texans in low- to medium-income neighborhoods. The "bank people" were cutting corporate costs by closing bank branches where the communities had less cash to deposit with them. Now the communities didn't have access to services like low-interest loans that could help improve their financial situations and instead had to turn to predatory, scammy options that inevitably worsened their financial situations. This same ruthless cycle was happening all over the United States in neighborhoods that already had history books full of predatory behavior from banks.

"Everything kind of came to a head around 2016, when we all started seeing the . . ." (Stephone paused, because there's no one right way to sum it up.) ". . . the killing of Black and brown people by police. And people were talking about using money to have an impact, and it was a new concept for me," he recounts. "There was this interview that [rapper] Killer Mike did on moving our money to Black-owned banks in Black communities, and I'm like 'Whoa, what is this?'"[3]

Stephone decided to start banking with Citizens Trust in Atlanta, but it admittedly took some work to find. The information out there was scant. While in the year 2000 there were about fifty Black-owned banks in the US, at the time of this writing, only twenty remain.

So, Stephone took to social media.

Letting curiosity lead him to find his people in the Twitterverse, Stephone and six new friends created a digital map that listed Black-owned financial institutions supporting Black individuals, homeowners, and businesses, calling it Bank Black USA. The resource has grown beyond anything they could have imagined in those early days of brainstorming, catching the attention of universities and popular culture media, and even winning "Best Graphic Design" awards for its aesthetic excellence.[4] Importantly, Bank Black USA makes accessible real conversations about banking history, culture, and accountability through digestible content so that Black banks aren't complicit in reinforcing a harmful financial system designed to serve only the few.

Today, Stephone is a national organizer with Hip Hop Caucus and sits on the board of the National Banking Association's Next Gen Advisory Council, helping ensure that minority-owned and minority-operated banks modernize their tech to meet the needs of communities. He still has the world's friendliest smile, has to wear reliable shoes on the job only on occasion, and knows that banks should serve the commons.

It's time the rest of our banking system gets the memo.

Banks Doing Bank Stuff

Banking as a concept exists to pool money and put it to work: rather than just sitting around, money brings in more money through the work of lending. For everyday people, the most common type of financial institution that we'll interact with throughout our lives is the RETAIL BANK.

First, retail banks give us a place to deposit our money in one location and then withdraw money in another. The US banking system is regulated by our pals at the Federal Deposit Insurance Corporation (FDIC), who insure the money individuals and businesses deposit up to $250,000 (e.g., in the unlikely case of a big bank heist at your branch).

Secondly, banks provide loans—personal loans, mortgages, auto loans, business loans, and more—through lines of credit and credit cards. They get to decide the cost of loans (i.e., the *interest rate*, which is the percentage charged by a lender on the principal amount borrowed, and *fees*, representing the cost of borrowing and the profit earned by the lender) and who gets to take out a loan based on a few factors like credit history, income, and collateral.

Lastly, banks provide customers with money-related services, like payment services, investment and financial advisory services, and currency exchange. For wealthy clients, banks also provide a suite of services that are often just called "wealth management"—personalized financial planning, investment management, estate planning, tax planning, and more to help them grow and protect their wealth.

Remember, when you think about the most well-known commercial banks, you're thinking of for-profit businesses. Yes, banks are regulated by independent government agencies, but they ultimately seek to make as much money as they legally can off their customers for their shareholders to pocket. That's just the business of (traditional) banking.

Bank Health Correlates with Community Health

It should come as no surprise that most unbanked and insufficiently banked individuals are from communities that have faced generations' worth of barriers.[5] For many, banks aren't the go-to option because they physically can't "go to" them. There just aren't any bank branches within a reasonable travel distance. Banking can be especially tricky for rural communities, which, in addition to a lack of physical branches, might lack reliable internet, making digital banking an incomplete solution.

Additionally, banks can and do turn down customers because of their current and past finances. Can't make the minimum balance to keep your

account open? Don't have the required identification documents? Have a poor credit history? The bank's playbook says they're not interested in doing business with you. This is especially troubling for people who may rely on government payments like disability benefits or food assistance that require a bank account where financial support can be safely deposited and accessed.

Beyond just not being able to access accounts, there's another reason why people don't take advantage of the services banks have to offer: distrust. Let's explore just a few root causes of this.

1. Banks Have Funded the Worst of the Worst Players in History

The banking industry came into existence to finance major business opportunities. Unfortunately for us, these major business opportunities included financing colonial settlers dispossessing Indigenous peoples of their land and resources, financing the trafficking of enslaved people and the industries that exploited them, and financing modern-day destruction of our climate by fossil fuel giants. Throughout history, banks have supported plenty of valuable, positive industries and initiatives as well, but to a much less significant degree.

2. Banks Love Charging Overdraft Fees

Fifteen billion dollars. That's the amount banks made from everyday Americans in overdraft fees over the course of just one year.[6] Every time someone tried to make payments that exceeded the current balance of their bank account, rather than automatically stopping the transactions from going through (which, yes, they have the capability to do), some banks heard "cha-ching" and tacked on fixed or proportional fees, like $35 per overdraft, or $5 for every $100.

This quiet tactic was so successful that, as revealed in one lawsuit, a Midwest Bank CEO named his boat "Overdraft."[7]

3. Banks Have Mismanaged and Stolen Wealth from Communities

Imagine piling your life savings in one place and then poof—it's gone forever. That's the kind of trauma that not only lasts a lifetime but can be passed on for generations to come. For example, the collapse of the bank Freedman's Savings and Trust Company "created justified feelings of betrayal, abandonment, and distrust of the American banking system among Black people that would remain in the Black community for decades," according to Mehrsa Baradaran.[8] That bank failure led to more than *half* of the community's wealth disappearing.

Internationally, people can point to the World Bank and its track record of funding certain projects in developing countries—including land grabbing, forcing displacement, and exacerbating poverty and poor health conditions through indebtedness—as a point of generational trauma. And let's not forget the 2008 financial crisis, during which some banks and lenders engaged in irresponsible and unethical lending practices, offering subprime mortgages to individuals with poor credit histories or low incomes while knowing perfectly well they would fall into a debt trap.[9] These mortgages often came with high-interest rates and hidden fees, leading to a high rate of foreclosures and massive wealth loss for families across the US.

4. Banks Have Been Straight-Up Discriminatory

Let's play Guess the Year.

A) When did it become illegal in the US for banks to discriminate against women accessing credit and financial services in their own name?

B) When were women entrepreneurs officially allowed to obtain business loans from the bank without requiring a male co-signer?

Check your guesses against the upside-down answer key.[10]

In addition to shameful histories of individual bank officers disproportionately targeting customers of color with exploitative products

A) 1974 (passage of
The Equal Credit
Opportunity Act

B) 1988 (passage of
The Women's
Business Ownership
Act)

Answer Key

like high-cost loans, fee-heavy accounts, and bad financial products, the problem is a lot bigger than a few bad apples making bad calls. Banks often use algorithms and models that inadvertently perpetuate racial and gender bias in risk assessment, resulting in the denial of loans or financial services to women and people of color.[11]

5. Banks Have Worsened Segregation and Limited Access to Opportunity

Redlining was the practice of banks systematically denying or limiting access to credit and financial services, like mortgages and loans, in neighborhoods of color. In the 1930s, the US Homeowners' Loan Corporation (HOLC) created color-coded maps of urban areas, categorizing neighborhoods based on perceived "creditworthiness" (i.e., the ability to be a customer that banks want to work with). Areas with high concentrations of Black and brown families were shaded in red (hence, REDLINING) and labeled as high-risk, no-go zones, making it difficult or virtually impossible for those residents to secure bank home loans and build wealth through homeownership.[12]

Even though redlining was outlawed in 1968, the ghostly generational effects continue to reverberate.

For example, in the bustling New York nineties, a young couple—a South Asian immigrant man and a white woman born and raised on Long Island—with a baby on the way was excited to purchase their first home in the suburbs of Long Island. The only problem was, when they would ask to see some homes that they knew they could afford in certain neighborhoods, realtors would tell them "Sorry, nothing's available." The homes they were shown were in low-income neighborhoods predominately made up of people of color, or at the obvious outskirts of white neighborhoods like where the woman grew up.

From time to time in the years following, the couple would wonder if discrimination had been at play. Those little suspicions were validated in November 2019, when *Newsday*, Long Island's local newspaper, released a big investigative journalism report called "Long Island Divided."[13]

The report exposed a major pattern of racial discrimination by realtors in the area for years. The investigation recruited testers—white and nonwhite undercover testers, who posed as prospective homebuyers and renters—to visit Long Island real estate offices and inquire about housing opportunities while being filmed by hidden cameras. Time and again, the realtors were caught altering what homes people were told were available based on their race.[14]

But why? Well, racism. But more specifically, because decades earlier, bank redlining had carved out white neighborhoods where property values were artificially inflated, and real estate agents (who work on commission) had a profit incentive to keep it that way.

The couple are just two people out of countless others who have felt the ramifications of a real estate market shaped by bank profit motives, decades after redlining's end.

They also happen to be my parents.

My family's stories are what ground me in the financial activism that asks institutions this question: Are you banking on us, or against us?

EXERCISE
What's Been *Your* Experience with Banking?

Do you recognize any of the harmful banking trends from your own life?

Has a trip to the bank been a joyful experience since childhood, or a nerveracking one?

How often do you check your bank account(s)?

No judgment, just an invitation to notice what's true for you.

Deciding where our money spends the night and what it's doing while there is one way to lay the foundation for power building. For that reason, let's make sure you're matched with your ideal financial institution(s) for both your own well-being and your community's well-being.

Know Your Options to Reclaim Banking

So, we know that saving and lending institutions have a lot of power over communities. They can also have a lot of power *with* communities—helping individuals and families protect, safeguard, and grow their savings in ways that have been inaccessible for those at the margins of society for generations.

Banks that are structured to maximize profit for a few shareholders before all else have no incentive to transform our financial systems to be more equitable. However, we can choose to support partners, including certified COMMUNITY DEVELOPMENT FINANCIAL INSTITUTIONS (CDFIs), that exist to fill the gaps and remedy the harms perpetuated by the traditional banking sector. According to the Institute for Local Self-Reliance, in 2018, community-based financial institutions held just 16 percent of the market share but made a whopping 52 percent of all loans to small businesses.[15]

Let's look at three of the most common alternatives to traditional big banks we can choose from.

Credit Unions

Just like retail banks, CREDIT UNIONS offer accounts to deposit your money, loan products, and credit cards. Very much unlike retail banks, they exist to benefit everyday people, not wealthy shareholders.

Credit unions are not-for-profit financial cooperatives owned by their members, who share something in common, like living in a specific community or working for the same company, often making the banking experience more personalized. For example, in July 2023 the sisters of Alpha Kappa Alpha announced the opening of FMO Credit Union—the first women-led, Black-owned, sorority-based digital banking financial institution.[16] AKA's membership is half a million women worldwide, who (along with their families) can now invest in and grow wealth with an economic institution that they collectively own.

ACTION
From Barbershop to Credit Union?

Read the story of financial activist Arlo Washington, who—after years of making loans from his Little Rock, Arkansas, barbershop—opened the state's first credit union since 1996, offering a blueprint for communities to create their own financial institutions.[17]

Oscar Abello wrote about Arlo's story for *NextCity.org*, a critical nonprofit news organization that's been curating undertold stories of marginalized people who are not only reimagining our future but also building it in real time. You might want to subscribe for their stories.

Because credit unions are designed to be accountable to community members and their well-being, compared to big banks these institutions typically offer favorable terms to benefit customers, including higher interest rates on savings and lower interest rates on loans. Additionally, they might offer specialized products and educational support to empower their members and encourage local businesses to thrive, and sponsor other organizations that are also giving back to the community.

Community Banks

Another alternative to big banks beyond credit unions is COMMUNITY BANKS. These institutions are locally focused and can be mission driven, serving the banking needs of individuals and businesses within a specific community or geographic area. That means they're likely to be smaller than a big bank but provide most if not all of the same basic services.

Beneficial State Bank is a community bank and the largest CDFI bank on the West Coast, serving communities in California, Oregon, and Washington State.[18] The bank's mission is to build prosperity in underserved communities—for example, by supporting housing projects while fostering social and environmental sustainability (e.g., investing in renewable energy projects). It is wholly owned in the public interest and a certified B Corp, which means Beneficial goes beyond just community banking and practices socially responsible banking.

Socially Responsible Banks

SOCIALLY RESPONSIBLE BANKS, aka ethical banks or sustainable banks, are financial institutions that incorporate environmental, social, and governance (ESG) criteria into their operations and decision-making processes. This means they aim to balance financial profitability with positive social and environmental impact (rather than putting one over the other).[19] They prioritize being transparent with their customers, investing in socially beneficial projects, supporting sustainable businesses, and promoting community development.

For example, Amalgamated Bank, headquartered in New York City, was established in 1923 by the labor union Amalgamated Clothing Workers of America (ACWA) to provide financial services to its members.[20] Because of this history, it is grounded in supporting workers' rights and social justice causes, and the bank is widely recognized for its labor-friendly policies and support of social change organizations.

Socially responsible banks are likely to serve a larger audience than a community bank, which may focus on just one geographic area. In general, they say no to working with industries that explicitly harm communities, such as through fossil fuel extraction, weapons manufacturing, or exploitative labor practices.

Start with Where Your Money Is

Let's take some pressure off: there is no perfect bank match, only what works for you and for communities in this moment.

If you don't currently have any bank accounts, it can be helpful to start by assessing your options for opening a checking or savings account. The good news is, you're never legally bound to a single financial institution: if you ever want to open a new account or bank with another institution, you can either close or keep your accounts. Here are some handy tools for narrowing down bank options:

- ◉ **MyCreditUnion.gov** for the US (self-explanatory)

- ◉ **MarilynWaite.com**, where financial activist Marilyn Waite curates a list of sustainable banks (as well as insurance plans, investments, and retirement funds) around the world

- ◉ **BankTrack.org** and **MightyDeposits.com**, helpful tools for checking what banks you want to stay *away* from for their bad behavior, and for helping you locate values-aligned alternatives

If you already have at least one bank account, ask yourself if you're satisfied with the financial institution your money's in and their treatment of the planet and underrepresented communities, or if there's room to find a more values-aligned partner. Look up if there are any active "Move Your Money" campaigns that activists might be calling for.

For example, amid the 2008 financial collapse, grassroots housing justice organizers called on the public to close their accounts at Wells Fargo and Bank of America in response to both banks' roles in the subprime mortgage crisis and upcoming plans to impose new extractive fees on customers. Activated by the Right to the City Alliance, 440,000 account holders switched to credit unions, and both Wells Fargo and Bank of America had to scrap their proposed fee plans.[21]

More recently, it became known that Wells Fargo was one of the banks providing major financing for the Dakota Access Pipeline (DAPL) project, which was planned to cross sacred Native American land and threaten the water supply of the Standing Rock Sioux Tribe and other communities downstream.[22] In a massive show of solidarity, protestors made sure to name the bank as complicit in the violation of Indigenous rights, the environmental degradation, and the ensuing police violence against those protecting the water supply. In total, banks that financed the pipeline lost an estimated $4 billion in account closings by customers in protest.[23]

When you find a new banking institution you're excited to support, you just contact them to get enrolled. There's no formula to approaching this new deposit relationship: it's up to you if you want to transfer all or just a portion of your money.

If you are having difficulty accessing any bank accounts, there's a good chance that others in your community are experiencing the same barriers.

With all its flaws, banking is still one of the most important systems individuals can use to save, grow, and protect financial wealth for themselves and their families over time. According to the Federal Reserve (the US's central bank), however, almost a quarter of American adults are either unbanked, meaning they don't have a bank account, or underbanked, meaning they have a bank account but still must rely on alternative financial services like **PREDATORY LENDERS** to meet their needs.[24] Not having a bank that meets your needs gets costly fast: whether you're dealing with cash or digital payment systems, bank account alternatives can tack on hefty additional fees to each transaction and exorbitant interest rates to the money you borrow.

Saving, lending, and borrowing outside of regulated financial institutions and legal protections comes with its own set of risks, but for generations, people have found ways to make it happen. For example, close-knit communities have maintained informal LENDING CIRCLES, where trust, reputation, and social ties play a significant role. In the best-case scenario, members support each other financially and foster a sense of solidarity, often without a profit motive and need for interest rates or collateral. Deciding whether you're comfortable lending or borrowing money from someone is something only you and your well-resourced nervous system can discern.

As a starting place, check out *MissionAssetFund.org/Lending-Circles*.

EXERCISE
Spot a Predatory Lender

Predatory lenders have business models reliant on trapping people in DEBT CYCLES: you borrow money from them, then can't afford to pay back the money plus the interest and fees they attach by the set payback time, so then you have to borrow more money, and so on. Here are some common red flags to look for:

◉ **You feel pressured.** When you say you need some time to think about the loan, a predatory lender might become increasingly pushy or "swear on [their] mother" that you can trust them (even though you just met).

◉ **High-interest rate + short repayment period.** In a move characteristic of payday loans, you're expected to pay the lender back in just a few weeks (aka by your next paycheck), and the annual percentage rate (APR) is uncharacteristically high. If the interest rate is in the triple digits? Run.

- ◉ **The offer seems too good to be true.** It's time to read the fine print. Predatory lenders are terribly excellent at hiding fees and balloon payments in the terms and conditions to make it challenging for borrowers to successfully pay back the loan.

- ◉ **You're straight-up confused.** You have the right to ask as many clarifying questions as you need to feel comfortable with your decisions. Anyone using confusing and complex language when trying to convince you to borrow money from them is likely not on your side.

- ◉ **When you search them online, you're not finding much.** The lender might not be licensed or regulated, which means there's no oversight or protections in play to stop them from being shady.

Again, it's important to remember that the root problem isn't people who take out loans from predatory lenders because they don't know better. The root problem is that predatory lenders exist to prey on those who have few other options. While educating ourselves on the red flags can be helpful, it's just one step in the bigger work of ensuring that people's financial needs can be met in less dangerous ways in the first place.

How I Opened an Account I'm Proud Of

Since I started working part time at sixteen, I've had a bank account with Citibank. There was a Citi branch in my neighborhood as I was growing up, it's the bank my parents have always stuck with, and I've had a generally good experience in terms of my personal financial needs. For ten or so years, Citi was the place where almost all the money in my life flowed in and out.

I started learning about the importance of community-focused financial institutions in my early twenties, but it took me years to finally open an account outside of Citibank. I had an irrational fear of "messing things up." Don't ask me what messing things up means, it was just a general feeling of not being financially confident. Plus, life stayed busy, and opening a new account wasn't something that made it to the top of my mental priority list.

What finally made me research alternative banking options, fill out an application, and open an account at a local credit union was this: I got a mini side hustle that came with a small new source of income. People were asking how I'd like to be paid: "Direct deposit? Where to?"

This "newness" opened my desire to want to easily track just how much these engagements were adding up to, outside of the savings account I've had since I was a kid entering the workforce. The sense of organizational neatness was *chef's kiss*.

I started the process by Googling credit unions near me, paying attention to the types of financial institutions I was physically passing in my daily life and coming across online, and, importantly, crowdsourcing from my local community. I posted the following on both my Instagram story and LinkedIn page:

> I'm committing to opening a new account at a mission-aligned
> financial institution by the end of the week. Drop your favorite
> #creditunion or non-trash #bank here! Thank you in advance![25]

... plus a few smiley-face-with-sunglasses and stack-of-money-with-wings emojis.

Notice how I made it timebound? Writing our intentions publicly can be a great tool for compassionate accountability.

I ultimately chose Self Help Credit Union, for a few reasons.[26] First, I knew it played an important role here in Oakland, as well as the other communities it has branches in. The credit union has a long track record of investing in residents and supporting well-respected community organizations. You are the company you keep, and Self Help had proven to be a trusted partner to organizations I see as trusted partners to communities.

Secondly, I realized there was a physical bank branch only five minutes from me. This was especially useful because they required the application paperwork to be submitted in person, though I knew

I would be able to access all banking services digitally through their mobile app and website afterward. The cherry on top was realizing they were located next to an amazing Black worker-owned grocery store, Mandela Grocery Cooperative, which always has both tasty food and the best music playing throughout the store. You know I treated myself after I handed in my application!

The minimum balance to open my new savings account was $5. I paid in all quarters. Not because I didn't have other options, but because I've had $5 worth of quarters on my shelf for way too long and I was excited to finally use it. Tanya, my teller, graciously accepted my coins and handed me back an informational welcome packet, congratulating me on my new role as a credit union owner.

I updated my invoices to include my new Self Help account routing number, and I've been visiting my savings from my mobile app ever since.

The Future of Banking for Collective Well-Being

Ready to help make an impact beyond your own personal account? You can advocate for organizations you're already connected with to open an account with an existing credit union, community bank, or socially responsible bank that overlaps with their location or mission.

5. Ask your community "What can we do together?"

By organization, I mean your workplace (whether it's a large corporation or a small business or nonprofit), your school, your place of worship, your family—anywhere that stewards money on behalf of members or employees to keep operations running. Remember, often the main reason that institutions don't already have credit union or community bank accounts is because *no one has ever offered up the idea before.* Until you.

If it's not a resounding "Yes, let's submit our account application right now," that's okay! Organizations are always balancing a lot of priorities, and setting a time to rediscuss the opportunity and a deadline for the institutional decision can be critical for getting the ball rolling. Even if the institution never ends up committing, you've done the work of educating and advocating about the power of community financial institutions.

ACTION
Influence Organizational Banking

The steps for helping open an organizational account are like opening your own personal account:

1. **Research community-focused financial institutions** that align with your institution's mission, values, and geographic footprint.

2. **Assess services and benefits**, making sure to lay out any fees, minimum deposit requirements, customer service offerings, and account features, as well as a track record of positive impact on the community.

3. **Contact the community financial institution** to ask questions directly: ensure that your institution meets the eligibility criteria and figure out what documents are required (typically tax identification numbers, business registration papers, and the like).

4. **Float the idea with other members of your organization**, sharing that you've already done the research and why you'd be excited to make this step toward investing in social impact and community development as a collective.

5. **Share your findings with key decision-makers**—ideally including the person or people who call the financial shots, like the chief financial officer, treasurer, and so on.

Public Banking—It's Happening

Banks that are designed to be accountable to everyday people rather than the pockets of shareholders? Sign me up.

Public banks are financial institutions that are run by professional bankers, who operate in the public interest through democratic institutions owned by we, the people. Their explicit objectives are promoting economic development, supporting social initiatives, and providing financial services to the public. That means **PUBLIC BANKS** might prioritize lending to sectors or projects that may not be deemed "profitable" to traditional Big Finance but are undoubtedly essential for public welfare—such as agriculture, small businesses, infrastructure, education, and housing. They can also play a critical role in promoting financial inclusion by providing banking services to segments of the population that have been underserved or excluded from traditional commercial banks.

Some well-known public banks include the State Bank of India (SBI) in India, KfW Bank Group in Germany, and the China Development Bank (CDB) in China. You may notice the US is missing. You are correct.

At the time of this writing, the US has exactly *one* public bank, the Bank of North Dakota, which provides low-cost loans to local businesses and farmers, as well as student loans and affordable housing financing, and has a track record of promoting economic development in the state.[27] But fortunately, the Bank of North Dakota isn't likely to stay lonely for long. With the help of dedicated financial activists, the tides are changing. In 2021, the US saw eighteen bills introduced in nine states and cities, in addition to the federal level, which set the groundwork for officially establishing public banks.[28]

ACTION
Sign and Share the "Friends of Public Banking Declaration"

From your trusty mobile device or computer, you can endorse the official declaration in support of public banks as an individual or on behalf of an organization: *FriendsOfPublicBanking.org*.

Public banks are a key piece of democratic infrastructure in a just economy because they mean that finances are owned directly by the people and dedicated to the public interest. As expressed by the Public Banking Institute (*PublicBankingInstitute.org*): "Public banks don't replace local banks. They partner with community banks to fill the gaps in our financial infrastructure [to] finance community needs such as infrastructure, green energy, affordable housing, and worker-owned cooperatives. And instead of supporting wealthy shareholders, public bank profits return to the communities they serve."

Just like no one person has to navigate the big bad world of banking alone, communities can partner with advocacy organizations whose work is to hold banks accountable. For example, over the past six years, the organization RISE Economy (formerly called California Reinvestment Coalition) negotiated agreements with banks to reinvest $50 billion into local California neighborhoods.[29] They're able to do this work in large part because of something called the Community Reinvestment Act, a US federal law that aims to combat the generational disparities caused by redlining by making sure banks reinvest in the low- and moderate-income communities where they take deposits.[30]

If your community lacks financial institutions that are designed for all to flourish (rather than for just a few to profit), connecting with banking advocacy groups is an invaluable first step to changing the landscape.

CHAPTER 6

Strategy 3, Flexing Some Buying Power

Among the great achievements of mass-consumption culture has been to convince us that what we have been conditioned to fervently want is also what we need . . . to the point that the nervous system becomes riled when the objects desired are withheld.

—DR. GABOR MATÉ,
The Myth of Normal[1]

In an **extractive** financial system, consumerism fuels the exploitation of people and the planet, manipulates consumers, prioritizes short-term gratification, and flows wealth out of local communities.

In a **regenerative** financial system, consumerism is right-sized to support people and the planet, empower consumers, prioritize long-term value, and circulate wealth within local communities.

By reclaiming how, what, and why we buy, we can collectively influence which businesses we leave behind in the extractive economy, and which will flourish alongside us into the future.

Take a deep breath (or three). Remember how I said the Playbook is a No Judgment Zone? This strategy prompts us to look at our spending, both personally and collectively. It also requires us *not* to do two things:

- Shame-spiral about our unhealthy buying habits (under a capitalist system designed for unhealthy buying habits).

- Fall into the trap of "conscious consumerism"—which tends to focus on individual choices and consumption habits—as the be-all and end-all to our financial activism.

Using this strategy *does* require a healthy dose of *discernment*: the practice of acting on the gut feelings we intuit and the knowledge we gain along the way. No two people use their spending power the same exact way, and sometimes the "ETHICAL" option to spend your money isn't so obvious. Flexing our buying power means making decisions that help us live more fully and feel less depleted, while simultaneously stewarding in a more just economy for all of us. If we act collectively, we can have nice things . . . and we can cut out the garbage disguised as nice things.

You may have heard the phrase "vote with your dollars"; that is, where you spend your money can signal the companies you support and want to see thrive. But that's just the tip of the consumer power iceberg. Shifting the way we spend money (how often, to whom, on what) has real implications for the survival of communities and cultures. It's a tool for pushing back on the trends that make us unwell (like OVERCONSUMPTION, manipulation, and unsustainability) and pushing forward on financial systems that help us reclaim well-being (e.g., through self-determination, reliability, and trusting relationships).

To borrow from the knowledge that emerged out of the 1960s and '70s feminist movement: "The personal is political."

Our spending is both deeply influenced by and indicative of social structures, power dynamics, and cultural norms related to our financial systems. So, before we hit "check out now," let's check out who we're doing business with.

How Overconsumption Is Written into Business Models

I have a personal "no Amazon" policy. (I also have a few times a year "Um, can I use your Amazon Prime account to get this really specific thing really quickly that I can't find anywhere else for nearly as affordable?" policy with my partner, who does have an account. As I mentioned, No Judgment Zone.)

Amazon has been a repeat corporate target of financial activist campaigns for many reasons, including but not limited to its decades of documented unethical treatment of workers, inadequate pay, anti-union efforts, mammoth tax avoidance, surveillance technology, data privacy concerns, unsustainable business model, and ungodly carbon footprint.[2] But my beef started with books.

While Amazon has contributed to the rise in self-publishing and potential audience reach for writers, it's also fundamentally changed the game by selling authors' work massively below retail price to dominate the market and incentivize people to purchase other items.[3] This practice knowingly puts independent bookstores (who don't have alternate revenue streams and a massive, overworked, and underpaid labor force) in a bind. Publishers struggle to maintain profit margins with Amazon having a lion's share of the international book market, which means they're less likely to "take a chance" on new (read: diverse) authors. The royalty rates on e-books have diminished for writers, impacting their ability to make income. And how viewable or high up a book is on an Amazon page is dependent on algorithms, resulting in a largely pay-to-play model for authors to even be discovered by customers.

How might this book business affect the well-being of communities? One salient example is when booksellers shut down because they can't compete with Amazon pricing. Physical bookstores leaving neighborhoods also means closing the door on gathering spots, event spaces, and cultural hubs for everyone from families with young kids, couples on dates, and elders who know learning is an endless journey. From a financial perspective, that means less foot traffic, less money circulating in the local economy, and less tax revenue back to the community.

The effects also manifest as a kind of dislocation from one another that's characteristic of our financial systems, like no more personalized recommendations from fellow perusers or employees. An extractive economy doesn't want us to truly see one another, contributing to the "loneliness epidemic" the US surgeon general has worryingly categorized as a public health crisis.[4]

The good news is, as much as it may feel like Amazon has completely taken over our options, book consumers have agency. For example, you might head to Bookshop.org, which is an e-store that supports real community bookstores in real neighborhoods with every purchase.[5] Or maybe you're someone who's already acquired more physical books over the years than can fit in your space (guilty), and you start a mini lending library (thank you to whichever neighbor first started the one in my building's third-floor laundry room!) Or you might pop by the closest public library, which exists to provide equal access to books (among a lot of other free resources) for everyone, or use your library card's barcode to access the whole catalog of e-books from home, digitally, using a free app like Libby.

The point is, the alternative solution to Amazon that communities need isn't one of us becoming a tech tycoon and building another Amazon-esque behemoth that's just slightly less terrible. The alternative solutions are all around us, sometimes as seeds hibernating underground, and sometimes already in full blossom and on display where we are.

While my staying committed to not having an Amazon account won't immediately change anything, it helps me keep strong the muscle of solidarity and join the countless others who are tending to community-driven alternatives for consumer wants and needs.

Buying Power

Buying power refers to the number of goods and services that can be purchased with a given amount of money, and is often used as a measure of a group's ability to influence trends in the market—for example, "the buying power of single-person households" or "the buying power of Latina moms in the US."

As a tool of financial activism, BUYING POWER can be tricky to reckon with. In a *Jacobin* article titled "You Can't Save the Planet by Yourself," Australian climate activist Philipp Chmel points out the ironies of trying to fight overconsumption with . . . overconsumption.[6]

"Today, more and more people define themselves—and their superiority over others—in terms of the products they buy," writes Chmel. "The choice for or against certain products can influence whether you are abstractly seen as a good or a bad person and can concretely spur self-judgment or condemnation of others. Indeed, not everybody can afford to participate in the ethical consumerism 'movement.'"

The shopping habits of everyday people aren't the root cause of climate change. The problem, in large part, lies with the mere one hundred companies that have been responsible for 71 percent of global greenhouse gas emissions since 1988.[7] The problem lies in policies that allow—nay, encourage—a financial system that lacks concern for the broader impacts of its actions. (Isn't that the definition of *sociopathic*?)

However, the shopping habits of everyday people like you and me *do* play a potent role in shaping the economy we deserve. Let's look at how.

1. Supporting Businesses That Thrive with Communities, Not at Their Expense

It's easy to think about products and services that aren't designed to promote collective well-being. But often, companies employ a deceptive marketing gimmick we'll call "impact-washing" that can make the discernment game challenging for consumers.

In the 1960s, the environmentalist movement started catching traction with the public, and it became sound business to at least *appear* to be environmentally conscious in order to not lose customers' respect. Companies started spending more time and money on crafting their images to be "environmentally friendly"—rather than spending time and money on actually minimizing environmental impact—to such a degree that advertising activist Jerry Mander (I know, no relationship to gerrymandering) called it "eco-pornography."[8] A few decades later in an essay about the state of the marketing industry, the term *greenwashing* was coined to describe the exaggerated and misleading nature of the hotel industry touting reuse of towels as proof of positive environmental impact.[9]

Today, this kind of "washing" to capitalize on growing consumer demand for socially minded businesses comes in all flavors (health-washing, rainbow flag-washing, feminism-washing, and so on).

ACTION
A Red Flags Checklist for Greenwashing

If . . .

◉ they clearly spend a lot of money on *telling* the public that they're good guys but have little to show for it beyond cosmetic changes;

◉ they don't engage with employees, communities they work with, or advocacy groups as a part of shaping business decisions;

◉ they regularly highlight their employee diversity, but it's not reflected in their leadership;

◉ they don't make it easy to track down how and where they source materials; or

◉ they have minimal data and reporting about their impact, and if they do, the reports focus only on how great they are (aka marketing material) with no mention of how they're committed to deepening their impact

. . . then they're probably **GREENWASHING**, impact-washing, you-name-it-washing.

For most of us, it's unrealistic to run through a checklist every time we want to make a purchase. However, practicing quick discernment can be a powerful force against marketing attempts to hijack social movements for financial gain.

Visual certifications on products, like "FAIR TRADE" or "B CORP" (an outside assessment of a company's practices and structures, like community involvement, environmental footprint, governance, and customer fairness) can be helpful indicators that a company is putting its money where its mouth is. Additionally, there are free apps and web browser plug-ins that empower consumers to know what they're buying. For example, the brand ratings system Good On You (*GoodOnYou.eco*) assesses brands for their impact on people, the planet, and animals. No tool is perfect, and there are plenty of companies that are doing great work that don't have external certifications or pages of public impact information, but it's a start.

Another tactic that's likely to increase our dollars doing more good than harm? As with banking, we can choose to put our money to work locally, preferably at independent small businesses and worker-owned cooperatives when they're available to us. Under our current financial system, many communities don't have the luxury, or basic necessity, of having safe, accessible, and diverse dining, shopping, and entertainment options. Especially in the wake of community economic devastation events (also known as "billionaires getting even richer" events) like the COVID-19 pandemic, small businesses shutter because of evictions and slow business and are then replaced by big-box stores that break down the cultural fabric of neighborhoods. Now more than ever, whenever possible, let's look for opportunities to keep it local and indie.

2. Spending for Your Financial Flourishing, Not against It

I don't love the identity of being a "conscious consumer." According to the Oxford Dictionary, one of the subdefinitions of *conscious* is to be "painfully aware of." *What would it look like to be joyfully aware, instead of painfully aware, of our personal spending?* And what would the impact be on collective well-being?

The psychology behind shopping is an interplay of cognitive, emotional, and social factors that influence our decision-making processes almost every time we make a purchase. From a profitability side, marketers often leverage the playbook of consumer psychology to create effective advertising and shopping experiences: instant gratification to give our brains a little dopamine hit, urgency and scarcity tactics to reduce our mindfulness, personalization to appeal to our sense of uniqueness, decision fatigue to push us into autopilot, and more.

Thinking back to the Trauma of Money, we each also have personal spending tendencies that arise from early cognitive patterns, survival mechanisms, and cultural upbringing. A time of high stress may show up in one friend as midnight online binge-shopping sessions for luxury products. It may show up in another friend as suddenly buying gifts for everyone around them while they struggle to make rent. It may show up in someone else as not spending at all, even while their stomach growls for a nourishing dinner and they have the funds.

So, across class, how do we begin to reclaim agency over our spending (and our nervous systems) under a financial system not built to see us thrive? We can start with a personal spending review.

EXERCISE
Run the Numbers, Feel the Feelings— A Personal Spending Review

You'll want ten to thirty minutes for this practice and some extra space to write on, but you can scale up or down as needed. You can also choose to do it alone or with someone else (for example, if you share a household with a partner). Might as well grab a snack, too.

1. Start by making a table with five columns, like so:

Purchase	Price	How I felt at the time of purchase	How I feel looking at it now	Would spend again? (Yes, No, Maybe)

---

2. Next, to the best of your ability, in the first two columns write out every purchase you've made in the last week, along with the price. You'll get this data from your credit and debit card statements, any peer-to-peer platforms you've used, and recalling where you spent cash. This doesn't include nonconsumer transactions, like donating or gifting. Also, it doesn't have to be 100 percent accurate—this data is just a snapshot to practice with.

3. Running down your list, recall how you felt at the time of the purchase (in a word, sentence, GIF—your choice). Was it a recurring bill payment for something you wish you didn't have to pay for? Was it something you bought spontaneously? Did the transaction happen on autopay?

4. Once that's done, list how you feel looking at each individual purchase now. Be open to whatever comes up.

5. In the last column, reflect on whether you'd hypothetically make the same purchase again (Yes, Maybe, No).

2. Check-in "How do I feel about this?"

We'll further explore the importance of reclaiming budgets in Chapter 10. But for now, you get to choose what happens next. Maybe you stop there and just give yourself credit for deciding what purchases you will and won't be making again. Or maybe you're on a roll and instead of just a snapshot of a week, you want to look at a whole month. You might find that you're comfortably able to maintain the traditional 50/30/20 guideline for personal budgeting: 50 percent of your income to needs (like groceries and rent), 30 percent to nonessentials (like dining out and entertainment), and 20 percent to savings and debt repayment (like paying off credit cards). Or you might find that ratio makes no sense because your current income doesn't even cover the bare necessities. Public service announcement: if you work a full-time job and it's impossible to cover your needs, it's evidence of employers paying below living wages. We'll address this later on.

3. Holding Companies Accountable to Progress, Not Perfection

If you were in America during the summer of 2020, you'll remember this: brands across industries posted messages of solidarity (to varying degrees) with the Movement for Black Lives, acknowledging the tragic police killings of Breonna Taylor, George Floyd, and countless others. Fashion designer Aurora James, daughter of a Ghanaian father and Canadian mother, remembers suspecting that companies didn't actually have anything tangible in place that could support the Black community like they were claiming.[10] As a business owner herself of the brand Brother Veilles (which sources handmade accessories from artisans around the world), she knew that Black-owned businesses were some of the first and worst hit as a part of the economic downturn.[11]

"Okay, here is *one* thing you can do for us . . ." reads the handwritten note she posted to her Instagram. Tagging companies like Whole Foods, Target, Sephora, and more, she wrote "[Black people] represent 15% of the population and we need to represent 15% of your shelf space."[12]

As of this writing, James has transformed the 15 Percent Pledge into a nonprofit that's worked with over twenty-eight major retailers. James's Instagram post asking for progress in actions, not perfection in words, would spur financial activism that's shifted almost $14 billion of revenue to Black-owned businesses to date.[13] Yes, that's billion with a *B*.

Around the same time as James's 2020 post, halfway across the world, other women working in the fashion industry—garment workers—were feeling the financial effects of the time. In our current international supply chain, factories often bear the heavy initial costs of production and wait months for reimbursement from powerful brands. However, when the pandemic struck, these big brands canceled orders and refused to compensate manufacturers for hours of completed labor, triggering a devastating chain reaction.[14] Over a million garment workers in places like Bangladesh, Myanmar, Cambodia, and Vietnam—many of whom were single mothers—were left abruptly unemployed with no financial safety nets.

Garment workers had already faced decades of union busting, gender-based violence, financial exploitation, and beyond-hazardous working conditions. In 2013 the world lost 1,138 Bangladeshis at the hands of corporate greed when the Rana Plaza—which produced for brands like Benetton, Zara, Primark, and Walmart—collapsed.[15] Now in 2020, brands tried to cut costs during the pandemic by leaving $40 billion in unpaid wages: eight years' worth of salary for *four million* Bangladeshi garment workers.

The message people sent these fashion brands in response was simple: pay up.[16]

Advocates organized by Remake and the Worker Rights Consortium (WRC) began confronting brands and published a Change.org petition, scathing report, and digital #PayUp tracker. Companies like H&M, Target, and Zara responded to the pressure pretty quickly, but the hashtag went viral when social media users pointed out that Kendall and Kylie Jenner's clothing line continued to be ensnared in the worker wage theft (the celebrities deny involvement). Influencers, meet influence.

The #PayUp campaign's impact grew, inviting a coalition of labor rights groups, NGOs, and everyday people to take part in putting brands on notice via social media. Over the course of two years, #PayUp succeeded in recouping around $22 billion (again, with a B) for suppliers, sparing countless jobs and securing livelihoods. Still, the work is just getting started.

"We will continue to hold brands accountable. We will continue with the campaign, empowering workers, [and ending] harassment and abuse in the workplace," shares Nazma Akter, founder of Awaj ("voice," in Bengali) Foundation and president of one of the largest union federations in Bangladesh. "We will [ask them to] increase the prices that directly impact workers' livelihood. We are pushing, always. We are continuing our fight. That is our journey."

4. Flowing Money to Ecosystems, Not Just Individual Businesses

3. Map "What's possible?"

Conventional business wisdom under an extractive financial system prioritizes competition at the expense of collaboration. Businesses may be so narrowly focused on selling their goods and services that they want to crush anything that might even potentially distract customers from hurrying up on the purchasing path. Talk about a SCARCITY MINDSET.

In contrast, we get to pay attention to the businesses that are already living into a sustainable financial system—which shows up as being collaborative in the spaces they share.

Charlese Banks, a business owner and brand strategist, describes the kind of collaborative culture she looked up to while growing up in San Jose, California.[17] "I remember my nail lady was connected to my hair shop. They had each other's backs—like you would go get your hair bleach, go [next door] and get your nail set, come back [to the hair shop]," she smiles. "They had this system, they would give priority to the customers so that they could get back in time. . . . Black business, Asian business unity, giving [each other] discounts and hooking each other up . . . you could create this flow in the streets."

If we were to drive about six hours south from San Jose, we'd find ourselves in Orange County, California. While both a conservative bastion and surfer's paradise, OC is also home to immigrant communities and communities of color who embody the definition of solidarity. There you might find Palestinian American Rida Hamida—community organizer, powerlifter, hot-pink hijab wearer, and founder of the organization Latino Muslim Unity—who describes herself on Instagram as "in a serious relationship with food."[18]

In 2017, Hamida's community was facing the heightened simultaneous demonization of Muslims and Latinos by Donald Trump's White House. Their response? Celebration and a call for taco trucks at every mosque.

Throughout Orange County, some taco trucks began serving halal meat—in accordance with Islamic dietary requirements and slaughter methods—and partnered with community masjids to serve locals. The scene is a racist's worst nightmare: Black Muslims breaking bread (or in this case, tortillas) with Latinx immigrants, Arab American kids playing with Asian American kids under the eyes of their elders, and everyone indulging a sense of lightness and unity.

"People think it's cute, a trend," Hamida told the *Los Angeles Times* about the #TacoTrucksInEveryMosque initiative. "But to say that is offensive. It's a way to dismantle systems that don't serve us." This community's power building is more than just coming together to eat: outside the taco trucks around forty thousand people have been registered to vote, approximately twelve thousand people received COVID-19 vaccines, and Hamida is preparing to host a summit to empower women to be financially free.[19]

Doing business with those who prioritize collaboration is a key tactic in building systems of shared wealth. Collaboration enhances stability, resilience, and trusting relationships within community ecosystems. Rather than the "divide and conquer" tactic of white supremacist playbooks, we get to spend our money with people dedicated to the tactic of "unite and build."

Reclaiming Personal Spending

Supporting businesses that we want to stick around into the next economy doesn't mean spending your own cash at every institution on every product or service. It can also look like curating small-business recommendations and good consumer deals you know others like you can benefit from.

<hr>

ACTION
Create a Patron Map for Your Community

Whether in the form of a note on your phone or something fancier (like a Google map with pins), you're going to want your patron map (aka your list of recommendations) to be easily shareable with others.

Think about the places where people can spend their money to have their basic needs and wants of all flavors met.

What's your criteria for assessing whether a place on your patron list is in line with "a regenerative economy"?

<hr>

Your list can cater to a wide demographic: those who have excess disposable income to spend, and those who don't at this time. For reducing waste, where are the secondhand stores and free markets? You might see if Too Good to Go, a mobile app that connects users with local businesses to rescue surplus food at discounted price points (usually about a third of the normal sale price), is operating in your city.[20] For a little bit of everything, you can also plug recurring markets or street fairs where attendees can buy directly from artisans, food producers, and more.

Get creative and specific. Are there any wellness businesses owned and operated by women of color you know are committed to redistributing wealth in their community? Are there restaurants that have been known to lend local organizers and activists their physical venues for events? What are the ethical products manufactured or produced locally, reducing the negative environmental costs of lengthy supply chains? And, of course, your recommendations can extend beyond the local and physical to products and services that can be accessed online.

As you try out new places, products, and services, ask yourself: Should this be added to the list, or what questions would I need answers to in order to feel good about adding it?

Be the Plug Small Businesses Need

Human brains are equipped with a fun evolutionary tendency that psychologists call "negativity bias"—giving more weight and attention to negative experiences or information than to positive ones. It takes roughly forty positive customer experiences to undo the damage of a single negative review.[21] Forty to one.

The ability to leave honest, transparent reviews (without censorship) on the businesses we give our money to is incredibly important. It equips others with more information, like instances of discrimination against folks of marginalized identities. Letting others know about *good* experiences as well can empower small businesses aligned with community wealth building to reduce their chances of being "written off" because of singular negative comments. Showing small businesses love on the interwebs is an easy but effective tactic to increase their visibility and, in turn, their cash flow.

By the power nobody vested in me, you're now promoted to Local Just Economy Establishment Ambassador for your community. Congrats!

Let's now move from an example of a personal financial activist tactic to an example of a collective financial activist tactic.

Boy Oh Boy(cotts)

Big institutions can support financial activists or be the very target of campaigns. One collective spending tactic used throughout social movement history has been the *boycott*: a consumer-driven refusal to buy or engage with a product, service, or entity to express disapproval.[22] It's the collective withholding of our dollars (which is different but often complementary to a strike—the collective withholding of labor by workers) in an attempt to make the powers that be and those standing on the sidelines pay attention.

For history buffs: the word *boycott* first appeared in the late nineteenth century, when it was used by Irish tenants in response to ruthless rent collection policies of an English land agent, Captain Charles Boycott. The angry tenants refused to work the lands and ostracized Boycott both economically and socially. The tactic has been used on an international scale to varying degrees of success, but it's particularly apt in societies where consumerism functions like a kind of religion.

As I write this, a news article pops up on my phone: Starbucks' market value has dropped a whopping 10 percent, which many suspect is a result of an international **BOYCOTT** in recent weeks.[23] When consumers learned that Starbucks union workers were being disciplined for sharing #FreePalestine posts in the midst of ongoing Israeli bombing of Gaza, they used the hashtag #BoycottStarbucks in about five thousand posts, garnering over 42 million views, according to the TikTok data center. That's correlated with an $11 billion loss for the company.

The lesser-known but equally interesting sister of the boycott is sometimes referred to as the **BUYCOTT**, in which consumers buy or engage en masse with an alternative product, service, or entity as a part of organizing.[24] In times of large corporate boycotts, we're reminded to show extra love to the local, sustainable, values-aligned little guys with our dollars.

The Future of Collective Spending

In a business context, the act of sourcing suppliers and purchasing goods or services from them is called *procurement*. But it can also look like planning a party.

Every cultural group around the world has found ways to celebrate life milestones, even in the hardest of financial times. We're talking coming-of-age ceremonies or rites of passage, graduation parties, anniversaries, religious calendar festivals, powwows, baby showers, and, of course, weddings. And families aren't the only ones looking to host a memorable event: the US corporate event market size is expected to reach $510.9 billion by 2030.[25] That's a lot of money flowing for trade shows, company galas, conferences, team-building meetings, and more.

If you're employed by or a member of an institution, look for PRO-CUREMENT opportunities that will circulate wealth in communities instead of just defaulting to the most known, "we've always done things this way" option. Every person has a circle of influence, and we get to be intentional about the ways we lovingly leverage that influence so that everybody wins.

Whether or not our pockets are overflowing with cash, we get to suggest and demand big spending toward the types of entities that will pour back into our communities.

CHAPTER 7

Strategy 4,
Giving (and Receiving) Money

*If we could use money in a different way, towards a healing,
reparative purpose, then money actually can be something
sacred, something that could be used as medicine.*

—EDGAR VILLANUEVA, *Decolonizing Wealth*[1]

In an **extractive** financial system, philanthropy is a tool of the wealthy to keep things as they are, reinforces unhealthy power dynamics, and is transactional in nature.

In a **regenerative** financial system, philanthropy is a tool for reparations and real systems change, empowers all involved, and fosters a sense of mutuality and sustainability.

By reclaiming how and why we give and receive money, we can generously fund the ease and fulfillment we've long deserved.

PHILANTHROPY has a problem. Or rather, it's operating exactly as it was originally intended, which is a problem.

In an episode titled "The New Gilded Age," *Throughline* podcast hosts Rund Abdelfatah and Ramtin Arablouei break down the origins of American philanthropy as "robber barons putting mom-and-pop shops out of business, and then turning around and saying they had the answers to cure poverty."[2] Rebranded as philanthropists, these powerful industry leaders of the late nineteenth century began using their unprecedented excess wealth—made possible by paying workers subminimum wages—to shape public opinion, indirectly prevent worker unrest or unionization, and strategically deflect criticism of their business practices and wealth accumulation. These philanthropists often donated to educational institutions with the aim of influencing curricula and promoting ideas that aligned with their own economic (ultra-capitalist) interests. In many ways, charity was a business strategy for keeping people in their place.

Here we are, over a century later. It's true that levels of philanthropic activity have increased in recent decades, funding amazing advances for society. But it's also true that the amount of wealth redistributed each year is pitifully small compared to the amount of new wealth that's produced and WEALTH CONSOLIDATION at the top. Tech executives are the new robber barons.

In his critically acclaimed exploration of the philanthropic field, *Winners Take All*, American journalist Anand Giridharadas put it this way: "There is no denying that today's elite may be among the more socially concerned elites in history. But it is also, by the cold logic of numbers, among the more predatory in history."[3] The class of people we call philanthropists have, by and large, reinforced the problematic notion that "society should be changed in ways that do not change the underlying economic system that has allowed the winners to win and fostered many of the problems they seek to solve."

This kind of corporate "Big Philanthropy" looks like foundations donating 5 percent of their annual assets to "save the planet" while investing 95 percent of their assets into extractive industries like fossil fuels (causing planetary degradation) and then being able to write off millions in taxes for charitable donations. It looks like only funding the *nonprofit industrial complex*, a system in which nonprofit organizations are dependent on catering to wealthy donors who deem what kinds of activism are "acceptable."[4] And it replicates the inequality so rampant throughout the rest of our financial system: as of this writing, only 0.5 percent of philanthropic funding goes toward women and girls of color.

However, Big Philanthropy is far from the only kind of giving we've got. "Most of what counts as philanthropic in the US (charitable gifts to tax-exempt nonprofits) comes from small gifts that are made by not rich people," writes Lucy Bernholz in *How We Give Now*.[5] For decades, unbeknownst to most of us, the vast majority of philanthropic giving—70 percent—has come from everyday people. We just don't always have the fancy galas to show for it.

With our role as everyday philanthropists in mind, let's explore what it means to give, and what it means to receive.

What Happens When You Ask for Support?

Desirae Callaway has called Colorado home her whole life.[6] Graduating high school a year early and going straight to college, she struggled to keep her grades up and found herself leaving college without a degree, saddled with student loans she didn't know how she was going to pay off.

"I ended up working as an exotic dancer for about two and a half years, just to make ends meet," she begins. "I'm also neurodivergent . . . and it makes it really hard for me to hold a normal nine-to-five job." When she was twenty-two, having just had her first child and realizing there would be no co-parenting or child support, a friend told her about an opportunity to clean some houses. "Do you want to earn some extra cash?" Desirae was listening. "And you can bring the baby with you." Desirae was in.

Clients would be surprised when she came ready to clean their house with a baby strapped to her back, but that surprise quickly turned to admiration for the quality and efficiency of her work. She did this for years. "By the time [my son] was three years old, I would just set him up with some early childhood educational games on my phone or something. So, he's learning phonics while I'm cleaning house—or if people would have their kids at home they'd be like, 'Yeah, your kid can totally play with my kids,' like a playdate. It was really cool, and I met awesome people like Addy."

Addy Lord is the mutual friend that encouraged me to connect with Desirae. As a neurodivergent mom herself, Addy formed a cross-class friendship with Desirae that went beyond employer and worker.

"Sometime during my second pregnancy, I was driving [my mom's old] vehicle that needed a lot of repairs, and I couldn't afford the repairs. [Addy and her family] had just bought a new vehicle, and they were going to donate their old vehicle. And so Addy proposed like, 'Hey, why don't we just exchange? For a few cleanings, you could have the car. There's nothing wrong with it, but it's older, so you could just use it or trade it in.'"

After a lot of open and honest dialogue, they mutually decided that what felt right was six cleanings in exchange for the car. "It wasn't like a charity thing where they're just like, "Oh, have this car for free, because we're like, wealthier people in this white area of town," Desirae laughs. "But it was more like, 'What would feel mutually EQUITABLE and doable to you in this exchange?'"

Months later, when Desirae showed up forty weeks pregnant with her second child to clean Addy's home, Addy gave her a larger check than what she owed her for that clean—a month's worth. "For all the cleans that you'll miss."

Addy—a watersheds, dams, and beaver-led ecosystems enthusiast, among many other things—knows that resources are multiplied when shared, and hoarding causes more harm for everyone. She grew up working-class before becoming wealthy and knew that benefits like paid maternity leave could be an out-of-reach luxury for the self-employed. "That was really nice, because it was unexpected. I didn't even ask for it; I hadn't even thought of it like that," Desirae remembers.

And then 2020 hit. "It was crazy. I was cleaning almost full-time at that point, and then all of a sudden, COVID shut everything down and people didn't want me in their homes." Desirae spent some time weighing her options. "Essentially, I was in a financial crisis."

Having skills as a seamstress, she started making and selling masks, which brought in enough cash for a month. But that business started to wane, and her tax refund was held up, so she was going to be short on rent. "It was really a bummer, because I had reached out to my landlord and was like, 'Are you guys doing any sort of like leniency on rent with the other renters because . . . it's a whole literal pandemic?'" she recounts. "They were like 'Well, nobody else is having trouble paying their rent.'" We both roll our eyes.

"So, I reached out to Addy. She had told me if I ever needed help with anything that she could help me with to let her know. So, she ended up loaning me the amount of my tax return until my tax return was processed, and then I paid it back in a couple of weeks."

Things were good for a bit. But then, as many readers might relate to, when it rains, it pours (and leaks, and makes you slip).

Desirae, her now-husband, and her children found themselves having to quickly leave the home they had been renting because the landlord's family was moving in. "I don't know if you know anything about the rental market in Colorado . . . [but for] a three-bedroom house, it's like $2,500 or more a month." That was about how much the five-bedroom house they had just been renting cost. "So, we're like, 'Let's see if we can buy a house.' I knew my credit would never get us a house, but my husband had decent credit and his work history was extensive and all that."

It turns out they could indeed buy a house, and they didn't have to put any money down: they were approved for a loan ("our interest rate was stupid") and Colorado Housing Down Payment Assistance. The family of five and their pets moved into a thousand-square-foot, three-bedroom, one-bathroom house, "packed like sardines," and grateful. It worked.

What didn't work? The one bathroom.

"It needed work done and my stepdad just happens to be an HVAC contractor," Desirae says. He didn't charge them for labor, but when the bill did come, the cost of bathroom materials totaled $10,000. (Around this time, Desirae also had medical costs from a slipped disc. And Christmas was right around the corner, and they were in the midst of getting presents for the kids.) "Yeah, it was a headache," she says with a tired smile.

As someone who had been reading "all the financial literacy" books and keeping ridiculously detailed budgets, she knew the costs it took to feed her family on a weekly basis, and that their mortgage was more than half of her husband's take-home pay. What she didn't have was the money to budget with in the first place. The couple started thinking about taking out student loans to cover the bathroom cost.

Desirae thought again about Addy, who had told her previously in no uncertain terms: "If there's ever an exact amount of money that would make your life easier, don't hesitate to call me."

"And, of course, I hesitated to call her," Desirae laughs. When she eventually did call, she shared the whole story with Addy. When Addy asked her "the number," Desirae told her. "She sent me a check for $10,000 and was like, 'This is a gift. There are no strings attached. This is how we're working together.'"

My jaw drops, but I'm not surprised Addy didn't mention any of this to me when she said I should connect with her friend Desirae. Her generosity tends to be understated.

"Asking for help was very vulnerable and new for me. I've always been somebody that can't ask for money," Desirae pauses. "I didn't feel like she was pitying me. It was more just like, she really understands the differentials, like the reasons that she has wealth and the reasons that I do not are fundamentally systemic. This was her way of supporting me and my family without like, checks and balances. Purely just a gift."

The bathroom got fixed promptly. "It was super helpful, and I'm forever grateful for that from her." Desirae lights up here. "And it inspired me to do a lot more work, a lot more learning and discovering, around my relationship with money and like, why I've always been stuck in this spiral of being lower, you know, *lower* working class." She also questioned why no one in her family had ever been able to make it out of the spiral of lower-lower working class.

"My husband is Black. I'm Indigenous. Nobody [in either of our families] had been able to accumulate [intergenerational wealth]," she shares. Desirae's great-grandma had to stop going to school in fourth grade to work in the fields. Her grandma was the first in their family to graduate with a high school diploma. Her mother was the first in their family to earn a bachelor's degree. And Desirae recently became the first person in her mother's line to receive a master's degree.

I think about the financial activist in front of me and the generational curses of inequity she is breaking. During our interview, her three children aren't home. They're at an Indigenous women–led, nature-based, trilingual summer camp, where they attend on a full scholarship. In her community, where families across class (low-income to ultra-high net worth) send their kids to the same programs, Desirae was one of two people involved in preparing a community meeting that would help parents with "getting [their] needs met while also meeting the needs of others" (Chapter 8 will talk more about **OFFERS AND NEEDS MARKETS**). She hopes that this kind of work can benefit all the parents she's in community with, making things "a little more efficient and a little bit post-capitalist."

Addy's collaboration with and investment in Desirae has returned back to her entire community. Desirae learned that her ability to ask for support was a radical act of care for generations to come.

Across class, our extractive economy doesn't want us to see each other. I'm reminded here of the Maya Angelou quote, "When someone shows you who they are, believe them." I'm so grateful that Addy and Desirae showed each other who they were—and believed each other.

EXERCISE
When You've Gifted, When You've Received

List two or three examples of when you *meaningfully financially gifted to others* within the past year.

_____

_____

_____

List two or three examples of when you *received a meaningful financial gift from others* within the past year.

_____

_____

_____

2. Check-in "How do I feel about this?" *Notice what you notice, feel what you feel, and keep that with you without judgment as you move through this strategy.*

A Just Economy Needs Community Philanthropy

3. Map "What's possible?"

Community philanthropy is a term I'm using to encompass the various models and approaches that aim to mobilize resources and engage community members in giving back to their local areas or affinity groups. It's long been present in communities of spirituality and shared culture, evidenced in practices like tithing in Christianity, zakat in Islam, tzedakah in Judaism, dāna in Hinduism and Buddhism, Dasvandh in Sikhism, kitty parties among South Asian women, potlatches in many Native communities, and so many more.

COMMUNITY PHILANTHROPY might include elements such as these:

◉ **Community foundations:** Nonprofit organizations that work with donors to manage and distribute grants to charitable activities in specific geographic regions

◉ **REPARATIONS initiatives:** Actions taken to address historical injustices—particularly related to systemic oppression, exploitation, and discrimination—typically involving compensation, acknowledgment, or the return of stolen wealth as a part of repairing relationships between groups of people

◉ **Online giving platforms:** Digital platforms and apps that enable community members to make small, individual donations to causes, nonprofits, or crowdfunding campaigns

◉ **Community-led MUTUAL AID groups:** Models in which communities themselves take the lead in identifying their needs, raising funds, and implementing projects that address local issues, like housing, food security, healthcare, and education

◉ **GIVING CIRCLES:** Groups of individuals coming together to pool their financial resources and make collective decisions about where to donate

Let's explore the last three in more color.

Online Giving Platform: The WellMoney App

As a Black trans man from Compton with dreads piled like a crown on his head, visible tattoos, and a T-shirt featuring the image of a brain (that's half realistic, half mechanical), Kortney Ziegler is a far cry from the tech bro aesthetic of Silicon Valley.[7] His many pursuits have all centered on innovations for liberating communities of color and queer communities from the constraints of "business as usual." He explains that while others are asking "How do we get rich?" he's asking, "How do we get well?"

"The pandemic was a moment for trust building. [People were] in the house saying, 'I just need $50,' tweeting threads of Cash App handles, and receiving stimulus checks that [showed we can just] give people money and they don't need to fill out an application or report back," Kortney shares. This period inspired the idea of a web-based, peer-to-peer gifting platform where all members can "share responsibility" in making sure people have a community to lean on when their car breaks down, they're short on rent, or they have an unexpected medical bill.

Enter WellMoney, his innovation to allow users to both donate and request support up to $200 for emergencies, with a sliding-scale monthly membership fee.

"Think about [a metaphorical] well," Kortney explains "where everybody can draw from it, everyone has access, and it's replenished by community support." (God, I love "money as water" metaphors.)

Unlike apps that are designed to keep you scrolling for hours until your eyes hurt, WellMoney is designed for efficiency. Filling out a request for funding takes less than five minutes, and the WellMoney team aims to review each request within forty-eight hours.

"We send cash directly to you because people deserve money when they need it . . . no need to share a personal story. Just tell us the purpose for requesting cash. We meet you with honesty and with trust."

4. Ask yourself "What can I do right now?"

Systems of giving that rely on a kind of Oppression Olympics for deciding who does and doesn't get funds ultimately work against power building in marginalized communities. They invisibilize the fact that financial scarcity is artificial and there's more than enough cash to go around among everyday people.

"Ninety-four percent of people don't 'take the money and run,'" laughs Kortney, anticipating the question before I think to ask it. "We're seeing people who receive money one month and then pay it forward 100 percent [the next]." We get to have each other's backs, and do so with ease and elegance.

A Mutual Aid Fund for and by Students

Grace Bassekle is a twenty-one-year-old student attending Carleton College, a private liberal arts college on a lush two-hundred-acre campus less than an hour from her hometown of Minneapolis, Minnesota.[8] A few facts about our new friend:

- ◉ Her parents immigrated from the small African country of Togo to the US before she was born.

- ◉ She's still figuring it out but is really drawn to the idea of being an urban planner.

- ◉ She's casually helped students redistribute wealth to fellow students over the past few years . . . to the tune of $20,000.

"It ranges from like medical bills to groceries . . . a couple of months ago someone's grandmother was going into hospice, so he needed to buy a ticket to go back home." Grace knows intimately the added stress of navigating finances in an unfamiliar environment. For example, she recalls with a giggle the awkwardness of trying to discreetly open her phone's banking app at the grocery store to transfer her last few dollars from her savings to her checking account to pay for food, juxtaposed with a friend finding another student's Amex Black Card (a card reserved for high-net worth individuals) laying on the ground of the dorm complex. Despite student pressure on Carleton (and its $1.1 billion endowment) to make the college more welcoming and navigable for low-income students, there are financial gaps the institution isn't willing to or cannot fill.

"When I was a freshman, Daunte Wright was murdered [by police] less than ten minutes away from my home," Grace recalls. "It was very devastating to me, because I [already] really had a hard time adjusting to college. . . . I felt out of place." Grace volunteered to help fundraise for a local community organization and was amazed at how the student body rallied to contribute about $10,000 in four days. People seemed eager to tangibly invest in something meaningful.

Recognizing the eagerness sparked by the moment, as well as the ongoing everyday needs of low-income students, Grace and fellow students established a donation fund with an easy digital payment system. Students are welcome to donate any amount, from a few dollars to a few hundred, which is then sent directly to low-income students who have applied for funds. What does this application process look like?

"So, we just check to see that [the requester is] an actual student at Carleton. And then we fulfill the request. It's very simple, in that sense," Grace explains.

Rather than having students attempt to prove their low-income status to qualify, the fund operates on a trust-based model. There's no judgment about how the money is used, no detailed report mailed out to everyone at the end of the year. Amid busy college life, the system was established to flow money efficiently, so that's exactly what the students do.

Grace sees the dignity in everyone, recognizing that we all have needs, and we all have privileges. "I'm from Minnesota, and Carleton is in Minnesota. For me, it's easy transportation to drive back and forth right now with my parents here. That's not necessarily the case for international or out-of-state students. So having that support system there is big."

Low-income students can be recipients of funding, and they are also welcome to contribute back. No one is locked into the identity of "giver" and "receiver." Outside of a formal process or institution, students get to show up for other students—acknowledging that, at least on this campus, people can stop pretending like there's not more than enough wealth to go around.

Hella Heart Oakland Giving Circle

A *giving circle* is a form of collective philanthropy in which a group of individuals pools financial resources and expertise to support charitable causes and nonprofit organizations. For Asian American women in Oakland, California, the Hella Heart Oakland (HHO) giving circle offers a "for us, by us" model of local philanthropy, with a particular focus on improving the health and wellness of refugees, new immigrants, and the greater community. The idea emerged among friends over drinks back in 2012.

"We're first and foremost family and friends," shares Huong Nguyen-Yap, who invited me to join one of HHO's weekly Zoom meetings and see for myself.[9] "The giving for us is an opportunity to gather and to support each other, but also support the community through our gifts to community."

Though I was meeting the group for the first time in Zoomland instead of in person, the community feel was palpable. Within minutes of our conversation, the multigenerational group of women had already breezed through inside jokes, welcomed in family members to wave hello, and assured me that one of the elders on the call, Karen Ijichi Perkins, makes the best sushi and gumbo in the world. The group has been meeting somewhat regularly (weekly and monthly) for years.

"I think it's important to note that we all have different backgrounds; a couple of us formally work within philanthropy," explains member Nicole Kyauk. Her day job is as a senior director of philanthropic services at the San Francisco Foundation. Other members, like Lisa Wong, come from a different part of the nonprofit world: public education. "For me, this group really helps me in the classroom . . . looking at the students who aren't the 'study hard and move ahead kids,'" Lisa explains. "I have kids who work at McDonald's 5–11 PM, and they come in [to school] totally exhausted. Why should they have to do that?" The giving circle is an outlet to grapple with both immediate needs and structural inequalities.

As they've pooled and donated over $100,000 to local community partners, they've tied countless memories to each grant. There was the time they gifted bathing suits to refugee and immigrant women who were going to Lake Tahoe for the first time. There was the time they supported the youth organization YR Media to co-host an intergenerational discussion with the Brotherhood of Elders Net-work about racial justice and cross-cultural solidarity in Oakland. They started by giving micro-grants to community groups with an explicit focus on Asian women and girls, but over time saw the power of staying flexible in their strategy. "We hosted a couple of virtual events around solidarity between Black and Asian folks in March of 2021," chimes in Jill Kunishima. "We were still in the thick of the pandemic but felt conviction that we should mobilize in some way given the current state of things. It was pretty incredible to go from a place of 'Let's just do something' to an RSVP list of over seven hundred people."

In addition to redistributing what individual members might be able to contribute, circle members also raise outside funds through cre-ative events—for example, attending a Golden State Warriors basketball game together. "We invite friends and family, and we're able to invite, you know, over two hundred, close to three hundred, people to be at one game and to enjoy a game together while fundraising for us," explains Huong. Giving circles come in all shapes and sizes. Some involve just passing around an envelope or bowl for cash and then collectively decid-ing how to redistribute it.

HHO is set up as a FISCALLY SPONSORED project of a nonprofit organization, Philanthropic Ventures Foundation, which allows the giving circle to legally receive tax-deductible donations and adminis-trative support while pursuing a charitable mission. They can also take advantage of things like company matches—corporate giving programs in which an employer pledges to match, either partially or in full, the charitable donations made by its employees. The core of HHO's work is pooling resources and making investments in organizations that aren't necessarily being funded by Big Philanthropy. "We knew that there was always going to be a disconnect around access to power and resources, and there was something really beautiful about community support-ing one another," says Nicole. "And there are stories that we remember so fondly where folks that received just a couple of hundred dollars, saying, 'I thought about philanthropy as an old white person [thing],'" she laughs.

"Just knowing for my kids, they have a community outside of me that they can trust and build with, there's just a beauty in that," shares

Huong. Nicole, whose kid's smiling face has just popped into her Zoom window, agrees. "I want [my son] to know I'm going to [these] meetings or gatherings to talk about how to support community. Oftentimes communities are in scarcity mindsets, so this idea of abundance is really important." Karen, whose dinner table is often the one the giving circle gathers around, reflects on their collective growth. "We had maybe one child [in the giving circle community] when we first started. Actually, none. Now we have seven or eight, they're in school, kindergarten, first grade . . . it's amazing," she beams.

"It just starts with a group of people, and people talking. Whether it be the mechanics of a 501(C)(3) or a group of old ladies doing a knitting circle, it's really up to the group of individuals," says June Sugiyama. "I believe they will find, like us, the relationships are even deeper and bigger than we thought they would be."

CHAPTER 8

Strategy 5,
Showing Up for One
Another beyond Money

Let us practice meeting our own and each other's needs,
based in shared commitments to dignity, care, and justice.

—DEAN SPADE, *Mutual Aid*[1]

In an **extractive** financial system, money has an outsized role in how we identify and create value, in reinforcing an individualistic culture, and in defining what's seen as a valid way to support others.

In a **regenerative** financial system, money is just one form of capital, our culture champions collectivism and strong social safety nets, and mutual aid is central to how we each belong to communities.

By reclaiming how and why we show up for one another, we make visible the existing networks of wealth all around us and open new opportunities for community thriving.

Who are these aunties in my house?

With a language barrier between us, it was a common question I kept to myself growing up. As she aged, my Dadi (grandmother) regularly seemed to have a rotating cast of other Bangladeshi immigrant women coming and going, warming up plates in the micro-wave, watching Bangla soap operas, and shooting the breeze (or spilling the proverbial tea) with an exchange of sly smiles. In addition to my immediate family and the occasional Medicaid-funded home health aide (who were always other immigrant women with big hearts), Dadi spent a lot of time on the phone or in the living room with people I just assumed we were somehow related to.

The COVID-19 pandemic disrupted things, of course. For Dadi her season of old age involved less time hosting visitors, and more time masked up in dialysis centers and hospitals. When she transitioned out of this lifetime in the midst of the pandemic, we knew her funeral had to be kept small.

In the room with her casket, I bent over to kiss her delicate head for the last time in a fog of silent grief. To both my surprise and deep comfort, two stranger-aunties appeared by my side, singing, crying, and praying for her—for us. Dadi was brought to the Jackson Heights Islamic Center, where hundreds of community members—already gathered in the streets for morning prayer—readily incorporated her send-off into their service. From there we drove to her final resting place on Long Island, where my childhood best friend joined us out-side at the burial. Friends and family had flowers and potted plants and sweets sent to our home; another friend donated in Dadi's name to Project New Yorker, a community-based organization that offers adult literacy, employment readiness programs, and skills-based training to underresourced South Asian immigrant women and youth in Queens. The void of social distance was filled with a creative abundance of care.

Over the course of these twenty-four hours, I experienced both immense grief and a renewed connection to community. I recognized that loss and liberation can coexist. And I was reminded: we get to show up for one another. There's nothing more powerful than that.

Mutual Aid

For communities of color and immigrant communities like my Dadi's, traditions of MUTUAL AID encompass the tools and principles of care that empower people to survive and thrive against the odds.

What does this seemingly nonfinancial strategy have to do with financial activism? Sort of everything. Extractive financial systems thrive when individuals and communities don't show up for one another, allowing the prioritization of competition over collaboration, myopic views of success, and resource exploitation in the name of profit to continue uninterrupted. This leads to the displacement of communities and the breakdown of traditional support structures. Powered by boundless SOLIDARITY, mutual aid, in all its forms, is a deeply human refusal to be swept away by forces of disconnection and fragmentation.

EXERCISE
The Five Love Languages of Strategy 5

Circle your love language[2] (in this work of living into a just, regenerative financial system):

- ⦿ **Words of affirmation:** Acknowledging someone's worth and gifts outside of how "productive" they might be

- ⦿ **Acts of service:** Lightening someone else's load (running errands, repairing something that's broken, cooking a meal, and so on)

- ⦿ **Receiving gifts:** Sharing tools, skills, and items (ranging from extra fruit from your garden to teaching someone else how to start a garden)

- ⦿ **Quality time:** Hosting and attending forums, gatherings, and events, such as virtual organizing meetings and in-person community markets

- ⦿ **Physical touch:** Standing hand-in-hand with other financial activists, tending to a world with future generations in mind

---

Common mutual aid tactics include resource sharing, skill and knowledge sharing, food distribution, childcare support, housing support, community healthcare and medical support, community gardens, disaster relief, legal aid, shared transportation, language and translation services, and so much more.

"Mutual aid projects are a manifestation of power," write Kelly Hayes and Mariame Kaba in *Let This Radicalize You.* "While many of us have our own self-care rituals, few have collective-care and conflict-resolution skills. Frankly, it is often easier to be dangerous to the state systems that we confront than it is to be tender with each other."[3]

Mutual aid asks us to do the hard work of being soft landing spots for one another—not out of self-sacrifice or tit-for-tat strategy, but out of recognition that our liberations are bound. How do you tend to, and let others tend to, the threads that weave us?

Beyond the Financial "Capital Stack"

In the world of traditional finance, the term *capital stack* refers to the combination of various types of capital used to finance an opportunity such as a big investment or real estate development project. Often presented as a bar chart, the CAPITAL STACK represents the structure or arrangement of funding for a project, layer by layer, with each layer representing a different source of capital.

As we know, mutual aid can involve showing up for one another in ways that generously flow and invite in financial capital as we build a more just economy. But capital—wealth that seeks to generate more wealth—looks like so much more than money. There's no definitive list, but here are a few examples beyond financial capital you may come across:

- ◉ HUMAN CAPITAL: The skills, knowledge, education, training, labor, creativity, and experiences possessed by individuals and groups

- ◉ PHYSICAL CAPITAL: Tangible assets such as machinery, equipment, infrastructure, and real estate

◉ **SOCIAL CAPITAL:** Social networks, relationships, and connections that provide support, opportunities, and resources

◉ **CULTURAL CAPITAL:** Assets such as art, literature, music, and knowledge of cultural practices

◉ **NATURAL CAPITAL:** The resources and services provided by the environment, including ecosystems, minerals, water, air, and biodiversity

◉ **POLITICAL CAPITAL:** The influence, power, and connections to decision-makers that individuals or groups possess within political and social systems

◉ **TECHNOLOGICAL CAPITAL:** The resources and capabilities related to technology, digital tools, and innovation

◉ **HEALTH CAPITAL:** Quality of physical, mental, and spiritual health and overall well-being

◉ **EMOTIONAL CAPITAL:** Individual and collective emotional intelligence, resilience, self-awareness, and empathy

Let's break these down using a capital campaign I'm currently volunteering with.[4]

Freeing the Land

In the face of the ongoing ECOLOGICAL CRISIS, the grassroots justice and ecology organization Movement Generation (MG) has boldly posited that people need dream spaces to nourish and restore relationships with the land and build organized communities—especially for people who are disproportionately affected by climate change, such as Black, Indigenous, POC, queer, disabled, migrant, and low-income communities.

In 2021, MG allies from the Sogorea Te' Land Trust were informed about the imminent sale of forty acres of land that had been held by a local family for more than a century in the East Bay area of Northern California, in native Bay Miwok territory. Through years of trusted friendship and collaboration, Sogorea Te' knew that MG had been looking for a home—a place to practice collective governance and hold space for movement allies, local and visiting.

With funds raised through private philanthropy, MG and Sogorea Te' Land Trust purchased these forty acres in December 2022, taking the land off the SPECULATIVE real estate market forever, and into COMMUNITY STEWARDSHIP. With the help of the Sustainable Economies Law Center, organizers created long-term agreements with Sogorea Te' for MG to base their work here.

Now, MG is raising an additional $1 million in donations in the form of a public campaign with the help of volunteer phone bankers. The $1 million will go toward the building of a tiny home and a yurt ($210,000), a greenhouse ($95,000), artist/mural work ($50,000), studio renovation ($250,000), maintenance and repairs ($205,000), fire mitigation and resilient landscape ($90,000), people-powered solar consultation ($50,000), and installing greywater systems ($50,000).

On this land, among lush cedar, redwood, oak, and walnut trees, MG envisions resilient gardens fed by rainwater catchment systems. In retro wooden buildings, they see future healing, gathering, and cultural spaces. They imagine children playing and growing together on sunny, rolling hills blanketed by native purple needlegrass and poppies. It will initially be called the Justice & Ecology Center: a first-of-its-kind community space for retreats, workshops, and strategy sessions for MG's wide network of organizers, healers, artists, and earth workers—all building capacity to guide communities toward a Just Transition from the extractive economy to regenerative local economies.

3. Map "What's possible?"

Ready to identify the capital stack?

◉ **Financial:** The funds raised through private philanthropy that enabled the Sogorea Te' Land Trust to purchase the land, as well as the funds being raised for the public campaign by MG

◉ **Human:** The knowledge, skills, and expertise of the members of Sogorea Te' Land Trust, the organizers from MG, and other collaborators

◉ **Physical:** The land itself, along with the buildings and structures, such as the tiny home, yurt, greenhouse, and studio

- **Social:** The collaborative efforts between Sogorea Te' Land Trust and MG; the connections, networks, and trusted relationships formed over years

- **Cultural:** The emphasis on Indigenous communities, cultural spaces, and envisioning a place for healing, gathering, and cultural activities

- **Natural:** The diverse range of trees (cedar, redwood, oak, walnut), the planned rainwater catchment systems, and the idea of creating resilient gardens

- **Political:** While not explicitly mentioned, the influence and connections of the individuals and organizations involved in securing the land and raising funds

- **Technological:** The reference to sustainable practices like rainwater catchment systems, solar consultation, and greywater systems

- **Health:** The emphasis on healing spaces, retreats, and wellness

- **Emotional:** The shared vision, dreams, and emotional connection to the land and its potential

Practicing Where You Are

Over almost-fancy charcuterie and reruns of *Insecure*, my local friends and I have a very informal clothing swap a few times a year, usually at my friend Brea's apartment. It's a chance to get rid of what we don't wear and refresh our wardrobes for free. But it's also a time to mitigate waste, honor changing bodies and seasons, hype each other up, and decide the best place to collectively donate the remaining items.

Of course, the impact may be more granular than, say, a coordinated national effort to reform bail or increase community development funding. But these are the moments that remind me that we—as women of color, young people, neighbors—can create new ways of sharing value without anyone's permission. We get to experiment, redefine, and reclaim wealth, while being both soft and radical, frugal, and abundant. Start with where you and yours are and build from there.

According to The Verge, there are currently seven thousand individual "Buy Nothing" groups across forty-four countries, from New York's Chinatown to a suburb of Reykjavík, Iceland.[5] I have friends who connected to these groups on social media and furnished their entire apartments with free furniture—and others who efficiently gave all their furniture away when it came time to move.

Think about moneyless tactics for building safety nets of care with questions like: How can I give something away to someone who could use it? How can I get something I could use from someone who might otherwise just throw it away? Is this article of clothing irredeemable, or can it be made good as new with some mending? Do I need to buy eggs every week, or can I invite some chickens to live in my yard and produce eggs for us in exchange for a sweet chicken living setup? (Okay, that one is a stretch, but definitely on my future goals list.)

The Future Is Mutuality

In the work of showing up for one another and building systems for collective thriving, it's vital to rethink not just *what* types of capital we flow, but also *how* that capital is exchanged.

For example, *time banking* is a structured system where individuals earn and spend time credits for services provided or received. Each hour of service is typically equivalent to one time credit, and participants can exchange these credits for assistance from others. TIME BANKING places an emphasis on equalizing the value of different types of services and can involve larger community networks. In Chicago, 76 members of the Kola Nut Collaborative (*KolaNutCollab.org*) have used time banking to exchange over 240 services over the course of 900 hours. With Time-Banks.org—the organization founded by the father of modern time banking, Edgar Cahn—you can earn credits by giving your time to help someone and then spending those earned credits to receive help in return.

Another group process that encourages mutual aid is the *Offers and Needs Market* (OANM), developed by the Post Growth Institute. Event

participants reflect, share, and connect about their knowledge, skills, resources, opportunities, and needs. Developed by Donnie Maclurcan starting in 2012, the two-hour experience is designed to "expand the sense of what's possible" and what we deem valuable, based on Indigenous practices, appreciative inquiry, and asset-based community development.

"[The Offers and Needs Market looks at] two fundamental human needs: belonging and a sense of safety," explains OANM Manager and Lead Trainer Crystal Arnold, who began working with Donnie in 2017.[6] "It's very different from something transactional like Craigslist. It's a relational experience." People get to both share offers and practice asking for support to meet their needs in a space designed for dignity and a level playing field.

Here's how it works:

1. A group of people—friends, strangers, neighbors, colleagues— come together virtually or in person.

2. A facilitator prompts reflection on the multitude of offers and needs that may arise. These include:

   o **Passions** around which people are offering or wanting connection—from the *physical*, like hiking or a meditation group, to the *conversational*, like climate change or decluttering.

   o **Knowledge and perspectives** that people are presenting or seeking—from the *insightful*, like recommendations for a good plumber or a deeper understanding of Islamic traditions, to the *instructional*, like how to set up drip irrigation or use gender pronouns.

   o **Skills and services** that people are offering or wanting to access or learn—from the *formal*, like graphic design or Spanish lessons, to the *informal*, like pickling vegetables or making origami cranes.

○ **Opportunities** that people are providing or seeking—from the *time-specific*, like a workshop on software for small businesses or being an accountability buddy for the coming month, to the *extended*, like a job opportunity or project collaboration.

○ **Resources** that people are offering or needing—from the *physical*, like a car for sale or a place to rent, to the *intangible*, like a categorized list of inspirational TED Talks or funding for a community initiative.

3. The Offers Market "opens." In small groups of four to eight, each person briefly shares *one* offer, along with the availability of that offer, location, and financial or nonfinancial cost (if any); see Table 8.1.

4. Once everyone has had a couple of turns, group members ask clarifying questions and make connections.

5. The Need Market "opens." Again, each person briefly shares **one** need with the group, along with the timing of that need, location, and cost they are willing to pay or exchange (if any); see Table 8.2.

6. Once everyone has had a couple of turns, group members ask clarifying questions and make connections.

TABLE 8.1. Tracking offers (adapted with permission from the Post Growth Institute)

OFFER (e.g., shopping delivery, tax assistance, car for sale, introduction to a good plumber, sci-fi film recommendations)	AVAILABILITY (e.g., anytime/ sometimes, emergency/fixed number, now/ future date)	LOCATION, IF NEEDED (e.g., city, town, suburb; virtual)	COST (e.g., $/€/¥/hour, fixed, barter, negotiable, free)

TABLE 8.2. Tracking needs (adapted with permission from the Post Growth Institute)

NEED (e.g., Spanish lessons, graphic design, support to navigate healthcare system, an accountability buddy, funding for community project)	URGENCY (e.g., urgent/ semi-urgent, non-urgent/ future date)	LOCATION, IF NEEDED (e.g., city, town, suburb; virtual)	COST (e.g., $/€/¥/hour, fixed, barter, negotiable, free)

And that's it, in a nutshell. There's power in simplicity.

"It builds confidence and an ability to trust others, especially for people who may be currently unemployed, underemployed, retired, or undervalued by the market," reflects Crystal. "For example, a stay-at-home mom who loves cooking can connect with a busy single person who would love help with meal planning and preparation." The OANM stimulates creativity and rewires habits rooted in scarcity. This experience has helped many as they heal from social isolation.

"Even for people with plenty of money, it can be deeply gratifying to look within and see the multitude of offers and then practice expressing your needs," says Crystal. "This practice becomes more essential in times of financial hardship or market turbulence." Community organizers from over thirty-two countries have been trained to use the OANM to take the pulse on what is needed and to see what underutilized resources are available.

One of my favorite things about the OANM is that it doesn't require a ton of time, resources, or prep: anyone can host one, and whether they're conscious of it or not, participants already show up with a list of offers and needs. They might just need some practice and encouragement sharing them out loud. For additional tools and to become trained as a facilitator yourself, visit *OffersAndNeeds.com*.

More than just meeting immediate needs, choosing to show up for one another is how we redefine the "markets" where we provide and access value. Now, take time to revel in the wealth around you and see what new possibilities emerge. If you don't have financial capital right now, what other forms of capital can you leverage toward making change?

CHAPTER 9

Strategy 6,
Shifting the Budgets

Poverty is a predictable consequence of how we create our policies. It's a consequence of what we choose to invest our common resources in and not invest in.

—SASHA ABRAMSKY, journalist and author[1]

In an **extractive** financial system, budgets are treated as just numbers, prioritizing cost-cutting over sustainability and well-being.

In a **regenerative** financial system, budgets are a tool of empowerment, prioritizing sustainability and well-being over short-term gains.

By reclaiming how and why we budget, we can joyfully reprioritize our personal finances—and build democratic control over collective finances—so that we can have all of our needs and most of our wants met.

Have you been drinking water?

Over the course of one day, there's no precise amount of water that any given person should drink—but there's a range we'll call "enough," which varies slightly for each person based on factors like age, activity level, climate, overall health, and other sources of hydration. You know you're in the "enough" zone when you can go about your day unencumbered, not bogged down by the disadvantages of dehydration (from annoying brain fog to dangerous levels of exhaustion).

Conventional wisdom affirms that the enough zone is about eight glasses of water a day, but again, each person can listen to their body and adjust their water intake. In some time periods and situations, that person might need more; in others, less. To be sure, people can do amazing things on less amounts of water every day—some estimates say that 75 percent of the human population is dehydrated either mildly, acutely, or chronically at any given time.[2] But dehydration to any degree is far from sustainable or enjoyable.

(A much tinier portion—let's say less than 1 percent—of the population is *over*hydrated, where they consistently take in more water than their bodies need. Overhydration—also known as water intoxication—shows up as various symptoms of unwellness, not that dissimilar to being dehydrated. It's also potentially deadly.)

Now, returning to the idea of our enough zone, imagine that every person has a personal spigot labeled "income" where their drinking water comes from each day. Each person has one designated drinking glass and access to their spigot eight hours out of every day. Everyone's drinking glasses are all roughly equal in size, marked with a clear line three-quarters of the way up the side of the glass. There are a few things that can happen at this magical spigot:

1. Your glass is not filled with any water.
2. Your glass is filled with some water, filling up somewhere below the line.
3. Your glass is filled with enough water, right at or above the line.
4. Your glass is filled with more water than it can safely hold, and the water spills over the top.

There's something important to note about scenario #3. Because we all share the same water supply, this "enough" option is ideal both for you as an individual *and* for everyone else, because it's the amount that makes it possible for everyone around you to get their fair share of water too. But let's imagine what your options are if your spigot flows like scenario #4: more water than your glass can realistically hold. Your most likely options are as follows:

⊙ **Save:** You can tip some of the water into another water storage container to save for later—a safeguard against future unpredictable circumstances, such as a time when you're thirstier than usual, when your spigot decides to stop working for a while, when someone bumps into you and spills your glass, and so on.

⊙ **Redistribute:** You can tip some of the water right into the cup of someone who's dehydrated to help them get enough.

⊙ **Spend:** You can tip some water into someone else's cup in exchange for something they have that you might need or want in return.

⊙ **Invest:** You can tip some water into someone else's cup, in the hopes that they'll pay you back with even *more* water than you gave them at some point in the future.

⊙ **Waste:** You can watch water spill over the sides of the glass and go "splat splat splat" onto the ground.

How does this watery metaphor flow into the strategies of financial activism? The process of understanding, planning, and crafting intentional decisions about cashflow is also known as *budgeting* (see Figure 9.1). With our "money in," we get to:

1. **Prioritize** needs.

2. **Add in** reasonable wants.

3. **Minimize** unreasonable wants.

⊙ *Needs* are the expenses (the items and activities) we spend money on that are likely to help us survive.

⊙ *Reasonable wants* are the expenses we spend money on that are likely to increase our well-being (helping us not only survive, but thrive) *and* are likely to either have little effect or in some way increase the well-being of other people and the planet.

⊙ *Unreasonable wants* are the expenses we spend money on that are unlikely to increase our personal well-being *and* are likely to have negative consequences elsewhere, contributing to the exploitation of planet and people.

BUDGETING (whether we're talking about a resource like money or water) can be an incredibly powerful tool for reclaiming personal and collective well-being. It's about *prioritization, not deprivation* . . . and it's time that we experience budgeting not as an abstract luxury, but as a helpful tool we're all free to access.

Now, we're all imperfect. There will be times where we spend our money on unreasonable wants that diminish personal and collective well-being. But we keep it pushin': budgeting helps us plan to limit bad investments and focus on optimizing personal and collective thriving.

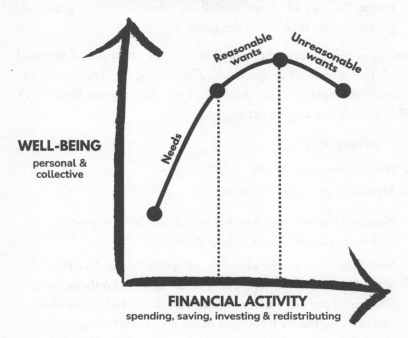

FIGURE 9.1. Finding the "enough" zone between financial activity and well-being

Budgeting also lets you see where the numbers just don't add up: if there's not enough money to go around, it's because someone(s), somewhere(s) is allowed to take more wealth than they could ever use in their lifetimes. It's because the cost of something fundamental to your survival—as an individual, business, or community—is tied up in financial markets and made artificially inaccessible and unreasonably unaffordable. Getting to the root of this mismatch is critical, and requires everyday people calling out the fallacies of prioritizing profit over people and putting real pressure on the players that facilitate inequality.

1. Question "Why is this like this?"

Whatever budgeting unearths, you have the agency and expertise to decide what the next best step looks like. I feel strongly that no single budgeting template will work best for everyone, but the practice (and it is always that, a *practice*) of making our money in and money out visible helps us pinpoint opportunities to reclaim wealth—who gets our money, where we may want to seek out alternatives, and to what degree our current income is meeting our current needs and future goals.

In essence, budgeting helps us meet our sense of "enough." So, what is enough?

Personal "Enough-Budgeting"

Using the basic data on our income and expenses, *enough-budgeting* is the practice of reflecting on, planning for, and resourcing our ideal quality of life, for every season of life. For my friends Ariel and Nathaniel Brooks, a married couple living comfortably in Western Massachusetts, tending to their household budget is the fertile practice ground for exploring "enough" in all aspects of life.[3]

"[Growing up, we both had] a lot of consciousness about money and standing on our own. We both worked a lot in college so that financial burden didn't fall on our parents," shares Ariel. Both recall growing up as the eldest children in families where there wasn't always enough money to go around. "I think about money as the freedom to direct your own time and put it towards other things."

Rather than having a set-in-stone statement to define "enough," Ariel and Nathaniel make it an ongoing process of inquiry. "We came to the idea of approaching 'enough' in terms of earnings targets by looking at [our] current cost of living. Doing a little bit of back-of-the-napkin [math], thinking ahead for aspirations around school and savings and retirement, and then coming up with an annual earnings target."

ENOUGH-BUDGETING for them is like running a family business—a business whose highest goals include connection, ease, and long-term sustainability. As we'll dive deeper into in Chapter 11, running a business, like being a part of a family, requires recognizing the things we cannot change while also focusing on the factors where there is real agency. As the only people who we can expect to tend to our own budgets, we get to decide what enough looks and feels like for us at any given time.

As working-class kids who met on a rich college campus, Ariel and Nathaniel today make incomes that cover their needs and most of their wants. Earlier in life, like many young adults, they basically spent what they earned, but they were careful not to accumulate debt. In their thirties, they started earning more than they needed to cover monthly expenses and were careful not to allow too much "lifestyle creep," especially in major expense categories like housing and vehicles. That means they have been able to save more, give more, and work fewer hours.

Over the years of attending college reunions, they've found themselves feeling grateful about the choices they've made when catching up with old classmates. "Other people are stressed out to pay their bills, even though they are in like high-powered, high-paying jobs," explains Ariel. "I'm like, I never feel stressed out to pay my bills, ever, which feels like a form of abundance. I never feel like I'm making constrained choices in terms of signing us up for activities or buying concert tickets, or if our daughter needs new gear. . . . I feel freely able to spend what I need for us to have what we need, knowing that the basic way we've structured our life enables that to be true."

There's freedom in clarity.

EXERCISE
Freewrite about Enough

2. Check-in "How do I feel about this?"

To enough-budget, we first need to give ourselves permission to name what "enough" even looks like.

Play your favorite song. For just the duration of the song, jot down what "enough" means to you. Read it back to yourself when you finish.

_____

_____

_____

_____

_____

_____

Speaking of freedom, last year Ariel decided to make a career change, from working within an organization to becoming an independent consultant. Before doing so, she and Nathaniel did some budgeting to find out a minimum goal of how much Ariel would need to make before having an impact on their family's current quality of life. And wouldn't you know it: Ariel hit that income goal with even fewer hours of contract work than she anticipated, freeing up more time than expected to volunteer and contribute to the local community.

"I'm only working part-time. So, I'm probably earning, like half of my potential earnings, but putting other time towards community things." Flourishing for her looks like the freedom to say yes and no to work opportunities, not maximizing as much money as possible just for the sake of it.

And for all of us, just getting by isn't the goal: it's the baseline. "We're in really wild times: we need to survive first, and we need to thrive first. It's not a contradiction, especially for those of us who grew up with less stability," asserts Ariel.

Let's cover some tips for honing your process.

Tip 1: Make It Easeful: Write Plans Down and Find Tools That Work for You

A budget can live anywhere you like: a treasured notebook, a digital spreadsheet, or even a ready-to-use template or app. "We've shifted to using Personal Capital (now called Empower), which is a free tool. We link up all our bank accounts, [which] can do all kinds of things like projections and stuff, pulling everything in," offers Ariel. The couple agrees that the more often they do this, the less overwhelming it feels, so they try to look at the tool, cashflow, and budgets at least twice a month.

Tip 2: Consider Collaboration: Who Needs to Be Involved?

The concept of approaching your personal "enough" budget like the most important business you'll ever run is useful whether you're a single-person household or a multigenerational family. Budgeting with trusted companions can be a gamechanger.

Unfortunately, we know that homes can also be a site of money trauma: 99 percent of domestic violence cases involve some form of **FINANCIAL ABUSE**, where one party uses access to finances as a form of control. Our money stories are significantly rooted in our childhoods, where themes like scarcity and debt cycles may leave lasting impressions that can take time and energy to unearth. But this is also true: home can be a site for reclaiming safety and well-being with your loved ones, whether they are related by blood, law, or spirit.

When I interviewed Nathaniel and Ariel, their daughter was on the cusp of turning ten. "We've been talking about starting to have a monthly family meeting where we actually look at the budget all together, what choices are made, and how that impacts our future planning." I know—getting adults to care about budgeting is work, let alone keeping a kid's attention. But the practice of enough-budgeting involves an embracing of imagination: daring to dream up what well-being looks and feels like.

Tip 3: Try Out a Monthlong Experiment

Approaching budgeting as an ongoing experiment is powerful. A timebound experiment, like just trying enough-budgeting for a single month, can build the muscles for longer-term planning.

"[I see it as an] experimentation with playfulness: what feels good?" offers Ariel. "[This month, someone could say,] 'I'm gonna try spending money on this one luxury, but like not these other things,' or 'I'm just gonna try checking my bank balance once a week and see what happens.'" You can try one experiment or multiple at a time to find what works for you, and tweak as needed.

Tip 4: Remember Your Community Needs You to Be Well

4. Ask yourself "What can I do right now?"

A financial system premised on overconsumption and profit maximization instead of optimization will never be in the business of helping people truly determine "enough": that is our work to do, and it's subversive work indeed.

I want to be clear: being financially stable or flourishing is not a prerequisite for meaningful contribution to movements. (I think about the decades of successful work by the Poor People's Campaign, for example.) At the same time, tending to our personal budgets reminds us that we are part of the "community" in terms like *community wealth building*. And if you're someone who has long lived in the land of abundance and your financial cup runneth over, the practice of enough-budgeting can enhance how you redistribute wealth both today and tomorrow.

When we individually operate in the enough zone, we create the conditions to keep burnout and resentment at bay, neither martyring nor resigning ourselves in the process. Hopefully, operating from enoughness creates abundance to share and fuel some of the earlier and later strategies described in the book, and it prepares us to participate in influencing collective budgets. Let's get into it.

The Future Is Popular Control of Governmental Dollars

Personal budgeting is one thing. Try asking some friends about governmental budgeting—and what being a taxpayer means to them—and watch how quickly their eyes glaze over, and how suddenly everyone begins whispering that you're an undercover fed sent by the IRS. Realistically, being a taxpayer can often feel like an inevitable frustration of this American life, rather than a point of democratic pride.

We're taught vaguely, if at all, that paying taxes is important: it fuels goods and services, like ideally non-potholey roads and firefighters with running firetrucks. Many of us also learn that the playing field of taxpaying is rigged: the ultra-wealthy often pay disproportionately less in taxes while most of us watch significant chunks come out of biweekly paychecks. The topic of taxes is a pain point across the political spectrum.

And yet.

Immense untapped potential for forging more equitable communities lies with simply claiming our status as taxpayers. It's one of our biggest mechanisms and secret weapons for change, and something financial activists are learning to hate a little less.

In broadest terms, when we're talking about tax dollars, we're talking about how, to what, and to whom a government allocates trillions of dollars in spending each year. What if, instead of finding this reality boring or intimidating, we found ways to make it interesting and joyful?

For example, in the summer of 2023, community members in Oakland learned that the Oakland City Council was planning on cutting significant funding to BIPOC small businesses.[4] The community said, "Not on our watch." Organized by REAL People's Fund (@realpeoplesfund on Instagram) and Network of Bay Area Workers Coops (NoBAWC; sound it out), everyday people were invited over social media to help make collective budget priorities known—through emails, public comments, testimonials, meeting requests with city council, and more.

5. Ask your community "What can we do together?"

As a result of everyday people's advocacy, the budget cycle ended up allocating $1 million extra to support arts and culture, fund grants for small-business improvements, activate economic corridors, and more. Not only were community members invited to participate in the actions, but we were then invited to Korner Kitchen and Bar to celebrate the win over delicious fried rice and noodles and fun drinks, at a party aptly titled "Small Biz, Big Energy."

From redirecting tax allocation locally (think effects on schools, affordable housing, and business investment) to nationally (like military and defense spending, foreign aid, and student debt), we've seen collective budgeting reallocation gain mainstream recognition in recent years. In the summer of 2020, for example, activists across the world called on American cities to "Defund the Police," a shorthand for shifting budgets away from bloated police and prison infrastructure and toward the severely underfunded line items of housing, education, healthcare, and more.

Similarly, the national organization the Debt Collective (*Debt Collective.org*) has been putting real pressure on the federal government to cancel household debts and reallocate taxes to fund college, housing, and healthcare for all. "Alone our debts are a burden," they remind us. "Together they make us powerful." As an often-overlooked but massively important financial activist movement, everyday people with debt have helped abolish more than $100 billion in student debt, medical debt, payday loans, probation debt, and credit card debt so far. Anyone can join the **DEBTORS' UNION** at DebtCollective.org and immediately access resources like a tenant power toolkit, events, actions, and (one of my favorites) the "B**** Better Have Our Money" student debt reclamation and dispute form.

ACTION
Watch "Your Debt Is Someone Else's Asset"

Search "Your Debt Is Someone Else's Asset" (narrated by Astra Taylor and illustrated by Molly Crabapple) on YouTube for six minutes and forty seconds of radically satisfying live art illustration, paired with game-changing statistics and tactics for collective debt cancellation.[5]

No matter their size, *all budgets are moral documents.* They lay out which values a given organization or government prioritizes. Some of the best tactics financial activists have at our disposal fall under the umbrella of a growing movement called *participatory budgeting* (PB): a democratic finance process that allows community members to directly engage in deciding how a portion (or all) of a government's budget is allocated.[6]

Participatory Budgeting 101

Imagine: in every city, everyday people—not politicians behind closed doors—regularly call the shots on what should receive more and less funding in our communities.

The first experiment of this kind was recorded in 1989, in the Brazilian city of Porto Alegre, where the local government turned part of the local budget allocation over to citizens and said, "Y'all figure it out." And the citizens did—helping reduce child mortality by nearly 20 percent.[7]

PARTICIPATORY BUDGETING didn't catch on in the US until around 2010, but has since grown exponentially, with hundreds if not thousands of district, city, or institutional processes happening at any given time.[8] Fostering transparency, citizen empowerment, and a sense of ownership over public resources, PB ensures that a greater share of community priorities shape budget decisions (see Figure 9.2). My first recollection of PB was a particularly scenic one: in pastel chalk on the ground near Oakland's Lake Merritt, someone had written out the city

how participatory budgeting generally works

FIGURE 9.2. The PB flow (used with permission from the Participatory Budgeting Project)

budget categories alongside an invitation to imagine how one might like to tweak it.

The Participatory Budgeting Project (PBP) is an instrumental non-profit organization that works to educate and provide resources, technical assistance, and expertise to local governments and community groups interested in implementing or expanding PB initiatives. To date, they've helped close to *eight hundred thousand* everyday people reclaim power over more than $386 million in public funding. Whether you live in a small town or big city, their website's informational resources can help users figure out what their taxpayer dollars are currently doing in their local neighborhood, and which elected officials they can contact to advocate for change.

PB isn't just happening at the city level. It's happening in schools, led by and empowering our youth—from Public School 139 in Brooklyn, New York, using parent association and school funds, to the Phoenix Union High School District in Arizona using districtwide funds. What makes PB as a concept so revolutionary is its ability to include *everybody*, including community members who may traditionally be barred from participating in democratic processes like general election voting.

"Whereas electoral politics typically engage the 'usual suspects'— higher-income, older constituents—PB engages traditionally marginalized constituents, including youth, formerly incarcerated constituents, and undocumented immigrants," writes Celina Su in her *Boston Review* article "Budgeting Justice."[9] In New York, she notes, nearly one-quarter of people who voted in the city's participatory budgeting process were not eligible to do so in typical elections. (Notably, since 2012, New Yorkers have decided how to spend more than $250 million on almost one thousand projects through PBNYC—making them the leader in PB activity in the US for the time being.)

"PB attempts to give stakeholders an opportunity to draw upon their knowledge of local needs, articulate proposals, interact with neighbors, deliberate over priorities, and select—not just consult on—which proposals receive funding," writes Su. Though far from perfect, PB is an avenue to real control over how our tax dollars are spent, with everyday people (not those beholden to corporate donors and real estate developers) in the driver's seat.

Let's see what might shift when the drivers change. Take a look at the two annual budgets for a community shown in Figure 9.3.

Budget Pie 1 is the actual budget put out by the mayor's office of Nashville, Tennessee, for fiscal year 2022.

Budget Pie 2 shows how nearly three thousand residents believed the city should spend their taxpayer dollars, as found by the Nashville People's Budget Coalition.[10]

By taking some of the existing money from institutions like these:

⊙ Metro Nashville Police Department

⊙ Davidson County Sheriff's Office

the city (as the everyday people surveyed saw) could free up millions for increasing investments into areas like these:

⊙ Affordable housing

⊙ Infrastructure and transport

Which budget pie would you prefer in your community? Why?

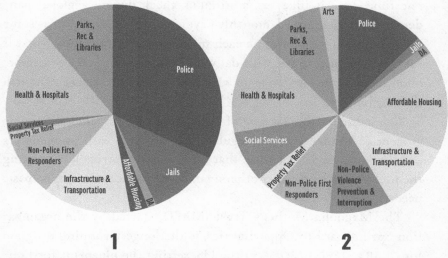

1   **2**

FIGURE 9.3. Two annual city budget examples

- ◉ Nonpolice violence prevention and intervention
- ◉ Social services
- ◉ Health and hospitals
- ◉ Education

Though the People's Budget wasn't implemented by the mayor's office, it's symbolic of a new era of organizing in financial activism: we're not just reimagining a slice of the pie, but questioning why we don't get a say on *the whole pie.*

"It's radical in the sense of amazing, not in the sense of unbelievable," shares Andrew Krinks, an organizer with the Nashville People's Budget Coalition. "[Everyday people] can determine the shape of our lives through budgeting and money beyond our elected officials."[11]

Getting to "Enough" with Guaranteed Income

What if you woke up tomorrow with an extra thousand dollars in your bank account? No strings attached. And what if this wasn't a one-time deposit (like say, a stimulus check during a global pandemic) but a guaranteed, monthly payment you could rely on as some soft padding to your income each month? And importantly, what if everyone you interacted with daily, and everyone in every neighborhood around you, also woke up with that same extra cash each month in their budget?

Guaranteed income is a type of policy tool that provides all eligible citizens or residents with a regular, unconditional cash payment. Its primary purpose is to ensure that no one has to struggle—harming themselves and sometimes others—in order to meet their most basic needs.

The Magnolia Mother's Trust (MMT), started by the organization Springboard to Opportunities, is the longest-running program for **GUARANTEED INCOME** in the US, setting the blueprint for hundreds of experiments that have since followed.[12] Every month for twelve months straight, low-income families headed by Black mothers living in affordable housing in Jackson, Mississippi, receive $1,000 cash. "[Our] early thesis was that if you diminish scarcity, local leadership will show up," shares Aisha Nyandoro, CEO of Springboard to Opportunities. "People needed breathing room to understand and question systems."[13]

The thesis was spot on. With additional cushioning, moms had the capacity to testify for better policies before local school boards and city councils. They formed intentional relationships with one another, trusting the MMT communities with their dreams and fears. Kids were surveyed: "How did this money impact you and your mama's life?" All data—both hard data and heart-centered stories—demonstrated an increase in the self-efficacy, sense of control and agency, and ease moms experienced over their day-to-day life.

"They think we're 'just giving moms money,'" Aisha says with a smirk. "Okay. Keep thinking that. What we're actually doing is transforming Mississippi power structures."

ACTION
What Does Wealth Mean to You?

In your family, community, or region, how might you define *wealth*?

For some inspiration on reclaiming the meaning of wealth and the budgets we use to manage wealth, give Aisha Nyandoro's twelve-minute-long TED talk "What Does 'Wealth' Mean to You?" a listen.[14]

(Snippet: "Asking more and more women the same question, I have come to learn that wealth is dignified funerals, the privilege of privacy, the ability to complete school, own a business, or the thrill of being the extravagant auntie. All of these are definitions of wealth to them.")

In these radical experiments of "free money," are we seeing people up and quit their jobs? Of course not. In many case studies, employment significantly goes up: those who received the payment were able to move from part-time to full-time jobs at more than twice the rate than those who didn't receive extra income.[15] Recipients often show a decrease in anxiety, depression, and overall stress, and an increase in health and overall well-being. The ripple effects of well-being meant fewer skipped doctor's appointments, more kids with school supplies and sports gear, less debt because of emergencies, and more care for everyone—not just the recipients, but everyone around them, too.

WEALTH REDISTRIBUTION is a way to put our best morals into practice, acknowledging there's enough to go around (for example, if we were to tax a mere 5 percent on multimillionaires' and billionaires' wealth, we'd unlock $1.7 trillion a year: enough to lift two billion people out of poverty).[16] It takes a concrete stance on the idea that everyone deserves the opportunity to thrive and access their full potential.

Let's revisit the thought experiment that opened this section. What potential might open in your community for collective well-being when everyone consistently has more in their budgets? What heights can we reach together when the floor is raised? I, for one, am ready to find out.

CHAPTER 10

Strategy 7, Leveraging the Magic of Investment

The goal isn't just to get by;
it's to live comfortably and have a
significant impact on the world.

—RACHEL RODGERS,
We Should All Be Millionaires[1]

In an **extractive** financial system, investing is a tool of the 1 percent focused on profiting from industries that harm people and the planet, moving wealth away from everyday people, and creating short-term financial gains without creating real value in the world.

In a **regenerative** financial system, investing is a tool accessible to the everyday person and focused on contributing to industries that support people and the planet, redistributing wealth that's been stolen through financialization, and creating long-term wealth building and collective well-being.

By reclaiming how and why we invest, we can redirect the flow of money away from corporate control and Wall Street, and into every-day abundance and Main Street.

---

*I*nvesting (verb): taking the initiative to endow someone with resources in the hopes of beneficial returns for them, you, and others over time. At its core, the equation is quite sensible: investing is an act of mutuality, where money in, plus time and activity, equals a strategic bet on more money out, and other real benefits.

So why does the investment industry feel so inaccessible and convoluted? Probably because the modern landscape wasn't originally designed for a moment in time like today, where everyday people (beyond land-owning white men) are allowed to participate.

In the United States, the first marketplace for INVESTMENT activity—Wall Street's New York Stock Exchange (NYSE)—was established in 1792, due in no small part to finance plantations of the American South and trade commodities produced by the stolen labor of enslaved Africans.[2] When the STOCK MARKET crashed and burned, precipitating the Great Depression of the 1930s due to unfettered investor greed, the US federal government stepped in. It created an agency to try to protect investors and the general public from another major financial failure resulting from market manipulation. This new agency, called the Securities and Exchange Commission (SEC), still makes the rules for the American investing game today alongside state regulators, calling the shots on who can invest, in what, and how.[3]

Fast-forward to the 1960s—set against the background of grand columns and a neoclassical facade, the NYSE's trading floor at 11 WALL STREET in Lower Manhattan was nothing short of organized chaos. Men in bright-colored jackets spent their days shouting, hand signaling, and running to make investments while a ticker tape printed stock prices and trading information on unending strips of paper.[4] (As the financial system evolved, so did financial activism: in one action organized by Abbie Hoffman and the Youth International Party, protesters threw dollar bills from the NYSE viewing gallery balconies onto the trading floor, briefly disrupting the trading activities and drawing attention to the absolute spectacle of Wall Street.)[5]

In more recent years, the NASDAQ stock market changed the game by introducing digital trading and INDEXES, which serve as a sort of benchmark representing the combined performance of the largest publicly traded companies in the United States.

Wall Street investing of today may appear tamer. But as market crashes and movements like Occupy Wall Street and youth-led climate change walkouts remind us, financialization wreaks daily havoc on people and the planet: exacerbating inequality, exploiting natural resources, and perpetuating a system of speculative short-term gains that redirect wealth toward the owning class and away from workers and real, tangible goods. This system is disguised in everyday language as the "investment landscape."

So, what do we, as everyday people who care about people and planet, do with this chaos? The financial system is hoping the answer is "nothing"—we continue to let the world of investing be dominated (and I mean *dominated*) by wealthy white men investing in extractive industries and laughing all the way to the bank.

Not on our watch.

Returning to the Just Transition framework, there are countless ways to get involved and "stop the bad" of harmful investing, as well as "build the new" with values-driven investing. In this chapter, we'll toggle between examples from all angles, exploring both personal and collective tactics to reclaim and redesign the game—building a society of regeneration, collaboration, and prosperous returns for everybody.

Starter Guide: An Overview of the Game

Please read the following required legal disclaimer in Dolly Parton's voice (it's just better that way): "The information presented in this book is intended for educational purposes only and should not be construed as personalized investment advice, honey."

Thanks, Dolly. With that in mind, let's review the game:

FINANCIAL ACTIVIST OBJECTIVE

Growing your money (to help secure a quality of life where all your financial needs and most of your reasonable financial wants are met), while simultaneously growing positive impacts for others (so that communities and the planet can flourish).

INVESTMENT TERMS TO CONSIDER

1. How much of a gamble you're willing to take with this money (RISK)

2. How much you're looking to make with this money (RETURN)

3. Ease and speed with which you might need to access this money and convert it to cash (LIQUIDITY)

4. When you'll need to "unlock" and access this money (TIME HORIZON)

5. The fee or cost paid for borrowing money (INTEREST)

6. How to spread out your investments across a range of different assets so you don't rely too heavily on any single investment (DIVERSIFICATION)

TWO MAIN TYPES OF INVESTMENTS

◉ DEBT (including loans/bonds/credit/fixed income)

- ○ **How it works:** Letting someone else (like an individual, a company, or a government) borrow your money in exchange for the amount you gave plus interest on an agreed-upon timeline. **Interest** is typically expressed as a percentage of the principal (original) amount.

- ○ **Example:** You lend someone $100 at a 10 percent interest rate for one year. At the end of the year, they pay you back $110, meaning your investment earned 10 percent, or $10.

◉ EQUITY (including shares/stocks/mutual funds)

- ○ **How it works:** Using your money to buy an ownership stake in someone's company or asset, getting money back if/when they make excess profit or sell that company or asset, or as dividends

- ○ **Example:** You buy a $100 share of a $1,000 company, making you a one-tenth owner of that company. The company successfully increases its value to $1,100, so its shares are now worth $110. You can either sell your share at the price of $110 ($10 more than you bought it for) or collect dividends if the company continues to grow. Dividends are a way that companies share their profits with the owners (*shareholders*) of the company.

Oh, and one more thing while we're covering the basics. Look out for something called *day-trading*—holding a stock for a few days or even hours. Day-trading isn't investing; it's gambling. The stress, risks, and downside losses far outweigh any benefits that your friend's cousin's roommate with one flashy watch may be touting. Not sorry.

EXERCISE
Inventory Your Current Investments

Lay out your current investments: how much money you're investing, in what kinds of investments, and for what kinds of value.

_____

Lay out any questions you may have about your current investments.

_____

_____

 Lay out a few of your investment-related goals: What makes them goals of yours (in the sense of personal well-being and wealth building)?

_____

Reflect: Are your investments meeting your goals *and* contributing to a more just economy for people and the planet? How might you even know?

_____

_____

It's important to remember that for all players, investing is a game of both strategy and luck. At the same time, the game is unquestionably rigged in favor of players who already have a lot of money. These players, called "ACCREDITED INVESTORS" or "sophisticated investors"—who, at the time of this writing, are those with over $1 million in net worth (excluding their primary residence), or more than $200,000 in earned income in the past two calendar years—have a different set of rules and access to more opportunities for bigger returns than other players.

The SEC's rationale here for this special privilege is that accredited investors can take bigger risks with their money in exchange for those bigger returns, which the average person can't afford. Which, in theory, seems kind of them to protect people from major loss. But let's face it: in reality the everyday nonmillionaire—or NONACCREDITED INVESTOR—is free to head over to Vegas and gamble away unlimited amounts of their money at casinos but is limited by the SEC when it comes to investing their money in businesses they care about and could benefit from. Sigh.

But as financial activists, activating everyday nonaccredited investors is our secret weapon. Taking more control over investing is a gamechanger—not only for building individual wealth, but also for reshaping the investment landscape. Let's get into it.

Investing in Our Future Dignity: Retirement Funds

People mostly invest because they want to save for big events, for big goals, for emergencies, and for the future. But the most common reason for investing is also the least sexy. We're talking about RETIREMENT.

Retirement accounts are generally invested in stocks, bonds, and mutual funds, and any earnings or capital gains from these investments contribute to the growth of the account over time. About 50 percent of US companies offer some form of retirement plan, and many also provide employer matching for their employees—meaning employers will contribute money to the employee's account up to a specified amount.[6] Literally free money on the table.[7]

So do me a favor: if you have an employer, find out if they have a retirement plan and matching program. Encourage your loved ones to do the same. The earlier you start, the more money you'll accrue. There's no such thing as a perfect formula here for how much to save, but a common tip is to start by saving 15 percent of your income (before factoring in taxes). You can adjust this amount as needed and may want to increase the amount the older you get. But if you realize with your income and expenses, you just *can't* strategically save for retirement, please recognize that this is a system failure, not a personal one.

In the US, we need deep organizing to fundamentally repair our retirement system, namely by instituting a mandatory savings system for all workers and/or expanding Social Security. "If we just taxed [the ultra-wealthy's] earnings like we tax everybody else's earnings, so much more money would come into the system and we could solve poverty and expand benefits," explains economist Teresa Ghilarducci.[8]

In addition to pushing for stronger retirement safety nets, it's also up to everyday financial activists to demand transparency and shift what retirement accounts are investing *in*. Currently, the majority of the most common retirement plans utilized by Americans—401(K)S—are invested in fossil fuels or weapons, unless the employer explicitly takes the initiative to screen those out.[9] Yikes.

Even in the case of companies who offer screens for their retirement accounts, the reality is that we're investing our future in public markets that extract wealth from workers and climate, further wealth inequality, and entrench corporate power and control over our communities. Systemic shifts in our economy and retirement system and the growing infrastructure for all of us to invest in regenerative, community wealth-building options will alter this reality.

Let's see how we can begin to ensure that our collective investments align with our collective thriving.

Shifting the Extractive Landscape of Public Market Investing

Everyday investors can buy shares of companies that are publicly traded on the stock market—aka public companies. The process by which someone might assess whether to invest in any given public company is referred to in investor-speak as *due diligence*.

EXERCISE
Practicing Due Diligence with EDGAR and friends

There's no one way to conduct **DUE DILIGENCE**. Everyone has their own style and approach. But if you're feeling like you have the time, energy, and curiosity to go deep on understanding a company, you're in luck. The SEC requires publicly traded companies to make available several key elements that could be important in due diligence, such as:

- ◉ **A basic overview of the company's business model,** typically found on a company's public website or annual reports

- ◉ **Insight into who's running the company,** typically found on the company website or in public annual reports

- ◉ **A picture of their financial health,** typically found in financial statements (like income statements and balance sheets) and cash flow statements (to evaluate profitability, debt levels, and liquidity, etc.)

- ◉ **A sense of industry dynamics,** like whether there is a growing or shrinking demand for the products the company makes, competition, and recent changes to the company

- ◉ **A sense of the company's impact on people and the planet,** including any reputational risks they might be facing. This is typically found in the press, media, maybe even the streets (especially when activists are the ones uncovering bad behavior from companies).

Much of this data can also be located through reports and filings listed the SEC's public Electronic Data Gathering, Analysis, and Retrieval (EDGAR) database.[10]

1. Pick a public corporation you recently used a product or service from.

2. Using Google, social media, or *SEC.gov/edgar/search/*, see if you can find one or two of the above data points that

an investor might use as a part of due diligence on that corporation.

Let's take a public company like Adobe, for example, whose stock ticker symbol is NASDAQ: ADBE.[11] Anyone with internet access can open an investment website and see the current value of each share. They can also learn a bit about Adobe's impact on people and the planet—for example, the fact that Adobe certifies that it has gender pay parity for all its employees across the globe.

Quantifying "impact on the people and the planet" can take on a lot of meanings—especially because impact is so nuanced. But at the time of this writing, in the investment sector the most common rating criteria for impact-on-people-and-planet is often shorthanded as ESG, which includes the following categories:

- ◉ **Environmental:** A company's sustainability efforts and impact, such as carbon emissions, energy efficiency, water usage, waste management, and overall commitment to environmental conservation

- ◉ **Social:** A company's impact on society and its stakeholders, including labor practices, employee diversity and inclusion, community engagement, product safety, and human rights policies

- ◉ **Governance:** A company's leadership, ethics, and transparency, including board composition, executive compensation, shareholder rights, ethical business practices, and compliance with regulations

Pushing for ESG Screens in Investment Funds

Conducting serious due diligence can be a lot, especially because most everyday people find their investments in *funds* of companies, rather than directly in companies. Funds are great tools for diversification, but the drawback is that they're often full of holdings that are terrible for people and the planet. So how do we know those funds are screening out companies with bad ESG ratings?

3. Map "What's possible?"

We might start by looking for funds that are ESG-high scoring by design, like the Nia Global Solutions Fund (NIAGX), which launched in 2022.[12] This is an active equity mutual fund that invests in about fifty companies with high scores in the areas of diversity and inclusion, sustainability, and/or social justice. I asked CEO Kristin Hull how one goes about actually getting a mutual fund that has verified positive impact into an employer–sponsored retirement plan.[13]

"As with all financial activism, it takes a strong voice for change, because the status quo of our systems is just so strong," Kristin says. Sometimes an employee can go straight to HR and say, "Here's this mutual fund I want to be able to access through my 401(k)," and that's it. That fund can now be an investment option.

Other times (and probably more often), you'll need to get employees onboard before HR makes it a priority.[14] And if you need statistics and talking points to support your request, try these:

- ⊙ "Did you know that only 1.4 percent of all of America's investments are managed by firms owned by women and/or people of color, even though diverse firms have proven to match or outperform nondiverse firms?[15] What's up with that?"

- ⊙ "Chances are that our retirement plan is currently investing 100 percent in funds managed by white men. That doesn't seem like a very good strategy. We can fix that."

- ⊙ "Here's a direct quote from Charles Schwab: 'There's no evidence that choosing ESG funds puts investors at any kind of disadvantage when it comes to risk or returns.'[16] Often, they have a *better* financial performance than non-ESG investments, because they're thinking about long-term benefit and not just short-term profit. Sounds like mutual fun to me!" (Sorry, I had to.)

As Kristin says, "We get the economy we invest in, and if everyone can just let that sink in and know that every dollar they're investing is contributing either to disrupting the status quo or to doing it in the same way . . . it's powerful. But it's going to take us being connected, talking to each other."

To further fuel our conversations, let's throw in two key financial activists' tactics that are powerful weapons for holding public companies accountable.

Shareholder Advocacy

Shareholder advocacy is an umbrella term for when individuals or organizations who own stocks in a company use their ownership to influence that company's policies, practices, and decisions. Shareholders engage with the company through means like meetings, proposals, and discussions to address issues they care about.

Here's why **SHAREHOLDER ADVOCACY** can be effective. Corporations want to minimize **MATERIAL RISK** factors—financial, political, reputational, and regulatory risks—in order to keep investors' confidence. If a corporation knows there's a material risk that could put its reputation in jeopardy but then fails to disclose that to its investors, the investors could sue it.

So financial activists can partner with qualified shareholders—any investor who's had at least $2,000 worth of stock in company for at least three years—to raise important issues by submitting a **SHARE-HOLDER RESOLUTION** or proposal, requesting that the company address the concern at hand.[17] Company management can then either meet with the shareholder(s) to negotiate a solution, which is usually their preferred method to keep everything looking fine and dandy, or they can let the resolution go into their proxy statement, which means that all investors can vote on it at the company's annual meeting. This can be high drama, both inside the room where it happens and in the press (in some cases, activists have staged and acted out mock shareholder meetings in the streets outside of actual shareholder meetings to garner media attention).

Key organizations like As You Sow, Majority Action, Corporate Accountability, the Interfaith Center on Corporate Responsibility, Little Sis, In the Public Interest, and Adasina Social Capital are just a few of the groups leading the charge, contributing insights and people power to hundreds of successful shareholder campaigns for change each year.[18]

Divestment

Another financial advocacy tactic, *divestment* goes beyond engaging with companies to actually ending relationships by selling or getting rid of investments due to ethical, social, or environmental concerns. A few famous historical examples of DIVESTMENT include the following:

- ⊙ **South Africa divestment:** During the apartheid era in South Africa, many individuals, universities, and institutions around the world divested from companies that operated in or had ties to South Africa.[19] This movement brought international attention to the issue and pressured the South African government to end apartheid.

- ⊙ **Tobacco industry divestment:** In the late twentieth and early twenty-first centuries, significant divestment campaigns targeted the tobacco industry.[20] Although they didn't lead to the collapse of the industry, they did impact its public image and influence.

- ⊙ **Fossil fuel divestment:** In recent years, a growing divestment movement has targeted fossil fuel companies. One example, Stop the Money Pipeline, is a coalition of more than two hundred organizations that has put real pressure on banks, asset managers, investors, and insurance companies to end ties with the fossil fuel industry.[21]

Okay, we know some ways to try to hold the corporate world accountable, which, under our Just Transition framework, falls under the strategy of "stop the bad." How do we take it a step further to "build the new"?

They say go big or go home. I say let's go big at home.

ACTION
Are There Human Rights Violations Hidden in Your Investments?

4. Ask yourself **"What can I do right now?"**

One of my favorite tools for understanding investments is the Investigate database hosted by the American Friends Service Committee.[22] There, you can search individual companies and funds to learn if they're complicit in:

- illegal land occupations or apartheid;

- weapons manufacturing;

- high-tech surveillance of migrants; or

- other heinous activities in the name of profit.

Investing in Place

"So, I purchased my first home when I was in undergrad—"

"Wait . . ." I cut in with a surprised chuckle, "first of all, that's unusual."

Adriana Abizadeh smiles at my confusion.[23] "It is very unusual!" she laughs in agreement. "And it's not to say that I was extremely financially savvy because that wasn't it. . . . I was unhoused for some time in high school. Rehoused myself. Started working and finished high school. [Became] salutatorian even having been unhoused for a good portion of my senior year of high school," she runs through her memory.

Adriana had an aha moment while paying rent in undergrad. "I was like, 'Yo, I'm paying these people's mortgage.' Like I'm legit buying somebody else their house and helping them build their own family's wealth," says Adriana. "And I was like, 'Nah, I'm gonna go buy a house; forget this!'"

Adriana went to the COMMUNITY DEVELOPMENT CORPORATION (CDC) in her neighborhood of East Camden, New Jersey. Like at many CDCs, she found a team of people eager to support her by offering down payment assistance, grants, or low-interest loans to first-time homebuyers, making the dream of home ownership more tangible (and affordable). While each one is different, CDCs often have deep neighborhood ties and can help first-time homebuyers connect with local resources and support networks and provide education on how to navigate government programs and incentives.

Becoming a homeowner at nineteen wasn't a cakewalk by any means; Adriana worked three jobs to pay her mortgage and put herself through school. But she describes knowing it was the right decision for her, as it grounded her in the stability and peace of having keys to a door she could safely walk through at her own leisure, every day. The experience also helped her realize that her sense of the financial system as unchangeable, unwinnable, and inaccessible to her as a single, low-income, brown woman couldn't be further from the truth.

"I think sometimes folks are like, 'It's just one house.' But that one house could begin changing [things] for your kids. I think sometimes we get [so] bombarded by the vastness of the system . . . that we forget that there's really small things that we all could be doing on the daily. They have impact. Everything has a ripple."

Reclaiming a Legacy

We know that hedge funds and private equity firms are always inventing hot new investment plays in the real estate industry. One of the newest involves bundling rent checks of everyday people into a package, and then selling the interests on those payments to investors for profit. Remember the last time we let Wall Street guys bundle a new financial housing product, back in 2008? Yeah. Now more than ever, we need innovative alternatives to defend and build local wealth.

In West Oakland before the mid-twentieth-century federal implementation of urban renewal policies, before the demise of shipyard employment and other good-paying jobs, before the repossession and destruction of Black-owned homes by eminent domain, and before railway construction ran right through the neighborhood, there was Seventh Street.

Remembered lovingly by Black residents as an illuminous "Harlem of the West," Seventh Street was home to bustling businesses, restaurants, and jazz clubs catering to longtime Black locals, new residents by way of the Great Migration, and famous visitors like Etta James, Aretha Franklin, and Duke Ellington. One of these jazz clubs, Esther's Orbit Room, is of particular historical significance. "Esther's was a big deal for Black art back then," recalls singer Faye Carol, who first performed there in the 1960s. "There wasn't a hell of a lot of places for us to perform outside of our own communities."[24]

5. Ask your community "What can we do together?"

But after this Black business district fell victim to disinvestment and the decision to use the right of way for a regional rail system, Esther's sat vacant for years. That was, until September 2021, when East Bay Permanent Real Estate Cooperative (EB PREC)—led in part for and by residents of the neighborhood—purchased the property and officially put Esther's back into the hands of the community.[25]

Buying Back the Block, Together

As a cooperative corporation, EB PREC is uniquely positioned to address the worst elements of the housing and development crisis. By buying and preserving East Bay real estate, it keeps tenants of color in the community, removes housing from the speculative market (forever), and publicly addresses the root problems of poverty concentration and neighborhood disinvestment.

How is it able to manage this project? By mobilizing the resources of both new and legacy residents, as well as outside investors, to help build collective wealth for more inclusive and equitable community development. EB PREC has a **DIRECT PUBLIC OFFERING** (DPO) of $1,000-priced shares that offer equity to purchasers in the community. And importantly, regardless of how many shares they own, every community investor-owner has a single, equal vote in governance—consistent with the cooperative principle "one member, one vote" that guides cooperative governance internationally. This gives tenants and investors alike the opportunity to flex the muscles of cooperative co-ownership and co-management, even if they have no prior experience investing in real estate assets.

Pooling investment money, sharing decision-making, supporting businesses that give back, and enjoying the returns is a recipe with the potential to transform communities and local financial systems— for good.

Similarly, in Northeast Minneapolis, a neighborhood of mostly working-class immigrants, community members began to brainstorm better uses for local, empty warehouses and formed the NorthEast Investment Cooperative (*NEIC.coop*). In this **INVESTMENT COOPER-ATIVE**, members pool their resources to collectively invest in various assets, businesses, or projects. "Each member put in $1,000. We used by-laws from a local grocery co-op, where $1,000 equaled one vote," shares my friend Michelle Tran Maryns. "[The cooperative] purchased and began to rehab commercial properties, buying our first two for about $280,000."[26] Return to the investors comes through rent from the underlying asset—the property—that is being leased to these businesses. In addition to a bike refurbishment shop, the buildings currently host Fair State Brewery (Minnesota's first cooperatively owned craft brewery) and Aki's Breadhaus (a German bakery). Equitable *and* delicious.

Investing in Community Enterprises

Think about a sports club, neighborhood cafe, or little-known artist you love. Now imagine that you and everyone else who loves them can be more than just patrons and fans: you get to invest in them.

For most of US history, it was very challenging for anyone other than accredited investors to invest outside the public markets—in startups, small businesses, and community projects. That began to change when Regulation Crowdfunding went into effect in 2016, with the primary goal of making it easier for unaccredited investors to invest in private enterprises (the more than 99 percent of the businesses in our country that are not listed on the public markets).[27] The updated regulations set into motion a new crowdfunding, or **COMMUNITY INVESTING**, framework that allows everyday individuals and organizations to collectively invest small amounts in businesses through online platforms. Though not (yet) widely known, this more democratic, emergent style of investing being built by financial activists is *loaded* with untapped potential for building sustainable community wealth and solidarity.

Community Investment Campaigns

Through digital platforms called *funding portals*, everyday people can explore open investment opportunities, learning the stories behind the businesses, and deciding whether they want to invest. Often, these can serve as a great entry into *local investing*, the practice of investing capital in the same region where you live, play, and work. "I think of LOCAL INVESTING as line-of-sight investing—you can actually see what you're investing in," says Arno Hesse, co-leader of Slow Money Northern California and co-founder of the platform Investibule. "There are other returns besides just multiples or financials. I mean, if people in your communities are employed, or you have good sources of good food and good services in your community. . . . That is quality of life for you. That means something to you. It may even bring up your home value if you own."[28]

EXERCISE
Imagine Your Local Community Investment Portfolio

From where we take our pets when they're sick, to who cares for the kids while we work, to where we make memories over romantic meals, chances are you'd rather have a local running the show then a faraway, faceless PRIVATE EQUITY FIRM that may know a lot about finance but very little about your community. Local investing lets us make our communities more vibrant while ensuring that the wealth we put in isn't leached out by absentee investors.

Given the opportunity, what local institutions you already know and love would you be excited to invest in?

_____

Crowdfunding is like a community garden: a lot of people tending to a lot of different plants, rather than just one type of plant that's susceptible to being wiped out if something goes wrong. It promotes sustainability and shared abundance, without requiring a tradeoff for quality.

Though early in its experimentation phase, digital community investing platforms are seeing greater dollars flow to the types of people mainstream finance either doesn't care about or doesn't understand—namely, women and people of color. Let's take Alicia Kidd, for example, founder of CoCo Noir Wine Shop, the Bay Area's first women- and BIPOC-owned wine shop.[29] In addition to working with traditional investors, Alicia invited her customers to become investors through an *investment crowdfunding* (or *community round*) campaign via the platform Wefunder. "I will be a multimillion-dollar business *and* I can have an equitable mindset," she asserts.[30]

Investment Circles

Another form of community investing happens through INVESTMENT CIRCLES and networks—groups that form to learn together and support one another—like Local Investing Opportunities Network (LION), Slow Money, and more.

One salient example is Invest for Better, a nonprofit that was formed to help women become confident investors who put their money to work in support of their values.[31] The organization works with women across the socioeconomic spectrum and has both nonaccredited and accredited members. In this model, eight to twenty women meet over a period of three to six months to explore their values, learn about impact investments across all asset classes (from cash through public and private investments to other alternatives), share insights, and build a trusted community. Over 90 percent of members report taking concrete actions to start moving their money into values-aligned investments within the first six months of their involvement.

Investing is a lifelong journey: Why not bring along and make some friends while you ride?

The Future Is Radical Investment Professionals

Black and Indigenous women, in particular, are on the cutting edge of investment futurism. Why? Because they've watched as the traditional investment industry has time and again undervalued their businesses and underestimated their communities. They're not waiting for saviors. Take RUNWAY (*runway.family*), for example, a Black- and brown-women-run financial innovation firm providing "friends and family" startup capital (also known as "believe-in-you" money) to overlooked BIPOC businesses. Or Native Women Lead, whose Matriarch Funds invest in Native American/Alaskan Native women entrepreneurs, recognizing that their businesses have managed to collectively generate $11 billion in revenue despite being one of the most underinvested demographics in the US.[32]

Money flows through relationships. Financial activist investors possess an emotional intelligence that allows for deep mutuality and a commitment to optimizing life for generations to come rather than maximizing profit over the course of a single quarter. Who's able to write the checks matters as much as who receives them.

And it goes beyond just investors. We need innovators all throughout the investment services industry—from accountants to advisors—reshaping the contours of risk and return. A deep understanding of the tools and rules at play is invaluable in the collective work of closing the racial and gender wealth chasms. Open source groups like Radical Planners have built a community of shared support, co-learning, and collaboration to help one another make the biggest impact in their pocket of the industry.[33]

The truth is that stepping into the role of investor, at any scale, can be intimidating. Or rather, the traditional financial industry *banks* on everyday people being intimidated, and therefore disempowered and leaving money on the table. To change the story of investing, we need to change the story of investors. What's your role in that change?

CHAPTER 11

Strategy 8,
Handling Our Business

These are the [working] conditions that exist,
but you don't have to accept these conditions.
We have the power to change them.

—DOLORES HUERTA, American labor activist[1]

In an **extractive** financial system, business exploits workers, builds wealth primarily for the owning class, and focuses on profit maximization at the expense of social and environmental impact.

In a **regenerative** financial system, business empowers workers, builds wealth for those creating value through their labor, and values the impact on people and the planet as much as it values profit generation.

By reclaiming how and why we collectively work (and don't work), we can creatively multiply flourishing beyond our wildest dreams.

Stripped down, BUSINESS is just the practice of how one regularly makes money. But today, "business" often comes with a recipe for resentment and burnout: workers find themselves in an economic system where work is no longer just positioned as a means to an end, but seemingly the end in and of itself. For the majority of people (for the majority of our waking lives), this practice involves active labor—producing goods, selling services, and so on—in order to meet our needs and strive for whatever it is we may want.

In *Work Won't Love You Back*, Sarah Jaffe reminds us that our extractive economy sells us a very particular idea of "freedom"—not *from* work, but *through* work.[2] "The ideals of freedom and choice that neoliberalism claims to embrace function, paradoxically, as a mechanism for justifying inequality. The choice is yours, but so are the costs for choosing wrong."

In other words, we give ourselves over to workplaces that promote teamwork, but not teaming up enough to organize for better conditions. That promote taking pride and owning the quality of our work, without actually getting to own our work products. That promote bringing our "full selves" to the office, while robbing us of sufficient time and energy to discover our full selves outside of work hours.

Combating the playbook of financial extraction, therefore, must be in service of a reality in which anyone is free to hand in a permanent resignation letter from being a cog in anyone's machine. Financial activism fights for a world where businesses should serve people and the planet—not the other way around. Let's look at how we get there.

"Be Your Own Boss"

The appeal of "being your own boss" is deeper than just not liking being told what to do. It speaks to the desire to be free from the exploitation so common in workplaces across virtually all industries. As a tried and tested tradition, entrepreneurship offers a foothold into this vision.

Naima McQueen is a business consultant and financial empowerment curriculum designer in her early thirties.[3] As a Black woman, Naima knows that Black women are the fastest-growing demographic of entrepreneurs in the US, having left corporate jobs where they're undervalued to chart their own paths.

"ENTREPRENEURSHIP is about community," she shares. "I think a lot of folks feel intimidated by entrepreneurship because they are convinced entrepreneurship is about the individual. But that is not in our history, particularly not as people of color. Our entrepreneurship has always been dependent on partnerships."

Entrepreneurship is also more than just profit-seeking and paper-work-savvy. "Statistically, [we create] businesses to fill a gap in community. What we do is art.... [Out of] scraps, we have created masterpieces."

Still, Naima cautions people against romanticizing entrepreneurship as the "best" or "only" path to financial wellness and generational wealth building. Founding, owning, and running a business is full of inherent risks. "We need to empower folks to do risk analysis. It's not just about the money, but the time, energy, and resources you put into it"—emotional, physical, and so on.

Today, an estimated 16 percent of all American adults identify as entrepreneurs.[4] But what about the rest of us? Naima used a term I've long thought about but never quite had the language for: INTRAPRENEUR.

Intrapreneurs are those who work *within* organizations to innovate new structures, advocate for change, and find creative ways to enhance collective well-being. "We need to honor that intrapreneurship is just as important and beautiful [as entrepreneurship] because we need people to do this work of community wealth building at every level," says Naima.

Keeping a business going also requires a lot of regular analysis—and your community needs you to not shy away from the hard work of looking internally. Consider: What work do you want to be doing? And perhaps more importantly: What do you want to be doing besides working?

"I realized I didn't want to wait to live my life at sixty-five years old. I didn't want to wait until I traditionally retired to be able to contribute to the world," reflects Naima. Fulfillment is our birthright, especially as human beings living in the wealthiest era of human history.

As we explored in the tactic of enough-budgeting (see Chapter 10), getting clear about how much income is *enough* at any given time in our lives is a critical first step to reclaiming personal agency. Parallel to thinking about what we need to earn, we also need to dream about what it is that brings us joy and fulfillment.

"I can go to urgent care and pay it out of pocket if they're messing with my insurance. That's the level of dreaming [I'm often stuck in] because I've been in survival and scarcity mode for so long," Naima admits. But when she's feeling nourished enough to think about what she really wants as far as income, it becomes clear. Her highest motivation is to enjoy life and contribute to community wealth building and well-being: the ability to give freely to friends and family.

"If I got it, they got it. I found that I needed to create an expense line for how much money I lend or give to my family members. [People may say,] 'Oh, why are you doing that? They didn't pay you back. People are taking advantage of you' and blah, blah, blah! And that's where I am. How I choose to make and spend money aligned with my values. It's rich auntie vibes over here."

That's her business. What's yours?

EXERCISE
Plotting What's "Your Business" in This Next Economy

Use the bull's-eye template in Figure 11.1 to clarify your values and identify "your business" in this next economy.

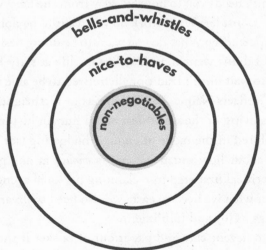

plotting "your business" in our next economy

bells-and-whistles

nice-to-haves

non-negotiables

FIGURE 11.1. This "bull's eye" is a values clarification exercise adapted from Swedish therapist Tobias Lundgren.

---

1. In the innermost circle, list two or three **non-negotiables**. What are you unwilling to compromise on for how you spend your work time (for example, the minimum annual salary you're willing to accept, the type of healthcare coverage you need and deserve, the maximum distance you're willing to commute, or how many hours a week of work is sustainable for you)?

2. In the middle circle, list two or three **nice-to-haves**. What are your strongest preferences for how you spend your work time (for example, the type of work culture you'd like to participate in, the level of autonomy you're interested in, the type of skill sets you'd like to use daily, or the ideal paid time off you'd like to have each year)?

3. In the outermost circle, list two or three **bells-and-whistles**. What would feel like a "bonus" to you related to how you spend your work time (for example, debt repayment support, paid travel opportunities, clear pathways to promotion, or a four-day work week)?

Remember, these are just examples; the answers will look different for each person. Honor what comes up for you when you consider these three categories.

4. **Now what?** Notice what made it into your circles. What needs to move? What's missing? What would it look like to pursue work in alignment with what you listed? What if you gave yourself permission to never settle for less than your "non-negotiables"?

When you're considering where and what you do for an income, this map is your tool to hold yourself accountable. Feel free to return to it on an annual basis, and notice what changes and what stays the same.

Financial Activism in the Workplace

Transforming how we work takes innovation, which means not only creating something new but also weaving newness with elements of the present and oft-forgotten past. Four powerful tactics that exemplify this process involve designing, unionizing, stopping theft in the workplace, and owning.

1. Claim the Right to Design

Despite all the forces that bank on our powerlessness and shape our understandings of what's possible, we are the truest architects of our own impact. Embracing the RIGHT TO DESIGN is a necessary foundation for changemaking.

Financial activists and researchers Joanna L. Cea, Jess Rimington, and a "co-learning community" of sixty practitioners identified a critical dynamic of how the dominant economy plays out: not only is financial wealth highly consolidated (i.e., a small group of individuals disproportionately reaps the financial benefits of collective work), but so is who gets to *design* how we work.[5]

Over the course of seven years of exploration, this co-learning community identified seven key practices that are a hallmark of enterprises successfully breaking out of business as usual and into forms of success that matter for all involved. Those practices, as outlined in Cea and Rimington's foundational field guide *Beloved Economies: Transforming How We Work*, are as follows:

1. **Share decision-making power** (e.g., by experimenting with a participatory budgeting process on an annual basis).

2. **Prioritize relationships** (e.g., by contributing to a community investment fund that connects place-based local funders with local businesses and community members).

3. **Reckon with history** (e.g., by paying land taxes to Indigenous stewards, and advocating for reparations initiatives that provide financial compensation and paid time off in honor of

communities who have survived systemic discrimination as a part of our financial system).

4. **Seek difference** (e.g., by implementing a community advisory board that shapes decision-making from a diversity of lived experiences, including across class and generations).

5. **Source from multiple ways of knowing** (e.g., by producing impact reports that prioritize qualitative data [verbatim storytelling] as much as quantitative data [numbers and statistics]).

6. **Trust there is time** (e.g., by practicing discernment in resisting the urge to treat low-priority tasks as urgent).

7. **Prototype early and often** (e.g., by testing out *profit-sharing models* and iterating on distribution methods and mechanisms over time to ensure fairness and effectiveness).

As laid out by Cea and Rimington, the workplace can and should be a space to "cultivate an awareness of the past and our present-day possibility for choice to undo harmful behaviors that have been normalized in the loveless economy." Remember, these practices aren't boxes to be checked—they're offerings to experiment with both regularly and simultaneously.

2. "Organize, Mobilize, Unionize"

UNIONS have a rich history as a force of financial activism, emerging as labor organizations in the eighteenth century in response to the harsh working conditions, low wages, and lack of worker rights during the Industrial Revolution. Gaining massive momentum in the late nineteenth and early twentieth centuries, unions continue to play a pivotal role in advancing economic justice, addressing income inequality, and securing essential benefits like healthcare and pensions for workers.

At the time of this writing, the American Federation of Labor and Congress of Industrial Organizations (AFL-CIO) is one of the largest and most influential labor organizations in the US, made up of sixty unions representing more than 12.5 million working people across various industries and sectors. According to their research, workers in a union have

⊙ higher wages (11.2 percent more than what nonunion workers make);

⊙ employer–provided health insurance (96 percent compared to 69 percent);

⊙ access to paid sick days (93 percent compared to 75 percent);

⊙ retirement benefits through private employers (82 percent to 48 percent); and

⊙ guaranteed pensions through private employers (54 percent to 8 percent).[6]

Though each union might have its own internal politics, drama, and limits to success, the aggregate data doesn't lie. Unions are a force for reclaiming collective wealth and well-being for working-class people.

What's the secret sauce? Their signature tactic is *collective bargaining*: the strength-in-numbers ability to negotiate with employers to reach agreements that determine wages, benefits, working conditions, and other terms of employment for their members.

Unfortunately, those behind rising income inequality have an anti–financial activism playbook of their own, and it's been effective: union membership in America has been steeply declining. There's a number of reasons for this trend. In some states, there are anti–union "right-to-work" laws that allow workers in unionized workplaces to opt out of paying union dues while still benefiting from COLLECTIVE BARGAINING agreements, intentionally weakening unions' financial resources and bargaining power.[7] At the workplace level, employers have actively opposed unionization efforts, with bold anti–union campaigns and practices that make it difficult for workers to organize, even outside the job. And as older, longtime union workers retire, they are often replaced by younger workers who may not have the same historical attachment to unions or grasp the scale of their importance. This is especially true as our economy has shifted from relying on manufacturing- and industrial-sector workers to big tech and gig work.

The good news is, we're seeing real bright spots that demonstrate why unions are just as critical in these moments as ever before.

For example, the Fight for $15 campaign began in 2012 when two hundred fast-food workers walked off the job to demand a higher minimum wage and union rights, ultimately winning at least $26 million in additional wages for workers.[8] In January 2019, over thirty thousand teachers in Los Angeles, represented by United Teachers Los Angeles (UTLA), went on strike for better wages, smaller class sizes, and more support staff in schools, successfully increasing teacher salaries by 21 percent.[9] In 2023, Amazon warehouse-workers-turned-labor-activists popped champagne outside the first successfully unionized Amazon facility, representing 8,300 people on Staten Island.[10] Perhaps most famously, in 2023, the Writers Guild of America (WGA), made up of 11,500 TV and film screenwriters we rely on for our Netflix binges, went on strike over an ongoing labor dispute with the Alliance of Motion Picture and Television Producers. I could go on.

And here I go. The graduate student workers' union at the University of Southern California won better pay, healthcare benefits, and improved working conditions; the National Football League Players Association (NFLPA) won revenue-sharing agreements and enhanced health and safety measures; Marriott Hotel Workers won improved contracts and job security; and the New York State Nurses Association (NYSNA) strikes won better nurse-to-patient ratios, workplace safety measures, and improved benefits for healthcare workers, to name a few.[11] Even my local Trader Joe's has unionized.[12] A subtle but awesome tip is to purchase a reusable canvas tote bag—depicting a fist clenching a box cutter and the campaign name stylized as the TJ logo—from the union Trader Joe's United website and use it to shop in store.[13] A financial activist statement piece, if you will.

ACTION
Find and Support Labor Actions

4. Ask yourself "What can I do right now?"

Even for those of us who aren't in workplaces where picket lines are happening, all industries are interconnected when it comes to worker rights.

A good starting place is to check out the Labor Action Tracker, an online interactive map maintained by the Industrial and Labor Relations School at Cornell University and the School of Labor and Employment Relations at the University of Illinois.[14] You can learn about worker demands (pay, healthcare, retirement benefits, etc.), access links to media covering the strikes and protests, and find out how you can lend support, in real time.

Also, here are some examples of labor action tactics beyond the collective bargaining we've already covered:

- **Negotiation/arbitration:** Workers collectively try to settle disputes and negotiate workplace conditions through discussion with employers before resorting to strikes or other actions.

- **Strike:** Workers collectively refuse to work until their demands are met.

- **Work stoppage:** Workers collectively disrupt normal workplace activities with sit-ins, walkouts, slowdowns, and other creative actions—like doing only *exactly* what the employee contracts or handbooks say is a part of their job.

- **Picket:** Workers collectively demonstrate outside the workplace to inform the public about labor disputes, unfair labor practices, or the need for support. Often with big ol' signs you can't miss.

- **Information campaign:** Workers collectively educate the public, lawmakers, and other stakeholders about workplace

---

issues and the importance of worker rights, using media outreach and social media campaigns.

◉ **Political advocacy:** Workers collectively endorse political candidates who align with their goals, using their active voter numbers as a bargaining chip.

◉ **Legal ACTION** Workers collectively file grievances or take legal action against employers for violations of labor laws or collective bargaining agreements.

◉ **Solidarity display:** Workers collectively support the goals of other unions or workers' movements because #solidarityforever.

◉ **Community outreach:** Workers collectively build alliances with community organizations, religious groups, and other stakeholders to gain support for their causes and leverage community pressure on employers.

---

3. Stand Up to Theft

What comes to mind when you think of stealing? Break-ins? Muggings? Credit card scams? As an estimated $50 billion problem each year, one quiet epidemic is now being recognized as the largest form of theft in the US—larger by far than burglaries, robberies, and car theft combined. It's also rarely addressed. That crime is the theft of worker wages by employers.[15]

"It's a way bigger problem that I think any of us have even the capacity to imagine," shares Rodrigo Camarena, director at Justicia Lab and the Immigration Advocates Lab. "WAGE THEFT means a number of things. Someone not being paid the right amount [they were promised], minimum wage violations, not being paid for sick days, or just straight up not being paid."[16]

Studies have found that foreign-born workers in some American cities are more than twice as likely as their US-born counterparts to experience wage theft.[17] "It's disproportionately impacting vulnerable communities like immigrants, women, and low-wage workers.... It's no accident that these are communities of color," reflects Rodrigo. "[Immigrants are] an entire labor force that this country has been exploiting since its founding. [We need to] think about the free riding that we're all doing on a labor force that is born elsewhere, is often educated elsewhere, gives us their most productive years, and then, when they're sick and all, go back to the country where they came from, in many cases." Rodrigo, who immigrated from Mexico to the US as a kid, knows the problem intimately. "As the child of immigrants, you just sort of grow up advocating for your parents. And so, my entire career has been in immigrant advocacy."

Bringing together other passionate immigrant advocates and organizations like Make the Road New York, data researchers, and workers who have been victims of wage theft, Rodrigo has helped facilitate "co-design sprints" to explore solutions for uncovering and filing complaints against wage theft. What resulted from this collaboration was ¡Reclamo!: a digital worker advocate tool designed to efficiently guide anyone who wants to help workers in the wage recovery process—community-based organizations, librarians, educators, and more—without needing to have a law degree.[18]

"[The ¡Reclamo! tool] gives them the confidence and the ability and the know-how to walk someone through the process of identifying whether they've had wages taken and recovering those wages," says Rodrigo. "[So far] we've helped file over a million dollars of wage theft claims. And we're super excited to keep developing and growing this project." The tool is now used statewide throughout New York, especially to support those working in the construction sector.[19]

It's no secret that low-wage, immigrant workers are often doing some of the most difficult jobs while systematically being robbed of the wages that they are lawfully owed. But the idea of fighting back can cause anxiety and confusion, especially if you are undocumented, face language barriers when trying to navigate mounds of paperwork, and are not interested in "rocking the boat" when providing for a family both within and beyond the country's borders. "People may feel that there's a lot of potential retaliation when engaging in the legal system; [they think complaining about stolen wages will] flag them for deportation," Rodrigo explains. (¡Reclamo! works to ensure workers' privacy is secured throughout the process.) "And so we have to do a lot of education and a lot of awareness building in the immigrant communities. That's why immigrant advocates are the key. They have the relationships. They have the trust of these communities. And so, we try to empower them and equip them with the material that they need."

"The technology is nice," smiles Rodrigo. "But the real innovation is in building that awareness and confidence in someone that doesn't need to be a lawyer to help file a wage theft complaint. The real innovation is in letting individuals know that they have rights. That they have power. That power needs to be exercised, and that others are trying to prevent them from exercising that power."

To be crystal clear: our laws say that workers who complain about wage theft cannot be punished for reporting the crimes against them. Advocates are working to build a financial future where skimping on paychecks and exploiting labor without repercussions is unthinkable. When we fight and innovate, we win.

4. Own It with Cooperatives

When it comes to the types of business models we'll need to power our financial activist vision of a just economy, we have options. Cooperatives, employee-owned businesses, and community-controlled infrastructure like land trusts all exist to promote economic democracy, local ownership, and self-determination.

They're also far from "new." As Jessica Gordon Nembhard comprehensively explores in her book *Collective Courage*, the *cooperative movement*—the development of businesses and organizations owned and operated by members who collectively share in the decision-making, profits, and benefits—represents a longstanding tradition in Black communities to pool resources, create businesses, and address systemic economic disparities.[20] In countries like Argentina,

Italy, Canada, Spain, and France, you'll come across thriving cooperatives—from Main Street small businesses to large agricultural conglomerates. You may even find hints of COOPERATIVE business in your fridge you never thought about—Land O'Lakes butter and Ocean Spray cranberry juice, for starters.

Let's imagine the different types of cooperative businesses that could exist within a single community:

- **A consumer cooperative** like a food co-op, where members (customers) collectively own and manage the grocery store, offering access to healthy and affordable foods and keeping profits within the community

- **A worker cooperative** like a childcare center, where employees participate in decision-making, share in profits, and have a say in the management of the business (including prioritizing job stability and income equality among employees)

- **A housing cooperative** like an affordable apartment property that's collectively owned and managed by residents, who encourage community engagement and call the shots on property management decisions

- **An agricultural cooperative** where local farmers come together to collectively market their products, purchase supplies, and share equipment and resources

- **A producer cooperative** where artisans collectively process, manufacture, and market their products—helping one another access larger markets, increase their incomes, and optimize efficiency

- **An energy cooperative** such as a wind farm that promotes sustainable energy practices, reduces energy costs for members, and generates additional income for the community

- And so much more, from coffee shops to tech hubs to credit unions and beyond

So, what makes supporting these businesses with our dollars and joining them with our labor so important? It comes down to the power of ownership: when the workforce owns instead of just works for businesses, more dollars flow directly to their families and their communities, rather than only "leaking out" to the usual suspects of financialization, who typically control the purse strings from afar.[21]

Employee ownership refers to a business ownership model where a company's employees hold a significant portion of the company's shares or equity, allowing them to benefit from the company's success and often participate in decision-making. If you've never considered **EMPLOYEE OWNERSHIP** as a pathway, think about this: according to Project Equity, profit margins of employee-owned companies are at least 8.5 percent higher than their competitors'.[22] According to a 2017 study by the National Center for Employee Ownership, workers in employee-owned firms earn 33 percent more than their peers in non-employee-owned firms, and their household net worth is a staggering 92 percent higher.[23] And as major economic downturns like the global COVID-19 pandemic showed us, businesses built on cooperative principles were more resilient, keeping more people employed and on payroll through the crisis when compared to conventional businesses.[24]

ACTION
Find and Support Worker Co-Ops

Worker cooperatives and democratic workplaces are vital building blocks of the next economy. If you're in the US, the US Federation of Worker Cooperatives and the Democracy at Work Institute maintain an online directory and interactive map of the fast-growing community of worker coops, other democratic workplaces, and support organizations—groups that together are advancing worker ownership across the United States.

You can access this resource at *USWorker.coop/directory/* to see what's happening in your local community (and maybe add some recommendations to your patron list from Strategy 3!).

At the time of this writing, about half of US businesses with employees are owned by baby boomers set to retire soon, most of them without a succession plan in place. This "silver tsunami" happening alongside the Great Wealth Transfer offers a win for all stakeholders when businesses transition to employee ownership.

As the Just Transition framework outlines for us, we get to transform work from a place of exploitation to a place of cooperation, as we shift our larger economy from one of extraction and scarcity to one of regeneration and abundance. It's our work: let's own it.

The Future of Work Is Well Rested

Deep in denial and on the frayed edge of work burnout, I stopped scrolling to read a LinkedIn post that began with this: "Pro bono Coaching for Professionals of Color." My first thought was "Pro bono means free, right?" I read on.

Transitioning from the financial services industry to professional coaching, Nicole Lopez-Conti—whom I had never met but was connected to on LinkedIn through a mutual friend—was rounding the bend to finish her certification and looking for two volunteers to help her fulfill her coaching practice hours requirement. Working with a professional coach was not something I had seriously considered before (or really understood), but I expressed my interest in learning more. Maybe Nicole could help me figure out this "work/life balance" thing.

A little over ten weeks later, my return on investment for saying yes to support surpassed my wildest dreams. As a coach, Nicole helped me realize that I thought a lot about work, but I had never carved out the time to assess my relationship to (rest)oration.

My homework was to form a consistent napping practice. To get clear about my boundaries—the distance at which I love myself and others. To luxuriate and let myself just be. By doing everything that I assumed would send me into financial disarray and instability ("there's work to be done and a world to be saved!"), I finally had the spaciousness to get clear about what I wanted and deserved for my labor. Soon after, I would secure a nearly $30,000 raise and promotion to a role that I designed for myself and actually wanted to do, while prioritizing ample rest over endless grinding.

I share this personal anecdote of deeply humbling fortune with two hopes in mind for readers of this Playbook. The first is a reminder that we often have more agency and opportunities for support than we may give ourselves the space to imagine when navigating our finances.

The second reminder is that when we resource, nourish, and honor ourselves with the gift of rest, new portals of possibility appear. Consider this quote from the nap bishop herself, Tricia Hersey, in her manifesto *Rest as Resistance*:

> Capitalism has cornered us in such a way that we only can comprehend two options.
>
> ⊙ Work at a machine level, from a disconnected and exhausted place, or
>
> ⊙ Make space for rest and space to connect with our highest selves while fearing how we will eat and live.
>
> This rigid binary, combined with the violent reality of poverty, keeps us in a place of sleep deprivation and constant hustling to survive. The work of liberation from these lies resides in our deprogramming and tapping into the power of rest and in our ability to be flexible and subversive. There are more than two options. *The possibilities are infinite.*[25] [Emphasis my own.]

In an economy that works for all, no one will have to choose between making enough money to stay alive and the divine right to rest.

Professional work and business activities can undoubtedly be a significant financial contributor to enhancing personal and collective well-being. From small businesses to multinational corporations, there's an abundance of opportunities and tactics for financial activists to shift capital (on larger scales than most of us can do alone) to communities who have been historically overlooked and intentionally exploited.

We also know that the types of work that pay bills and turn profits are wholly insufficient on their own in sustaining healthy societies. Care workers outside of formal workplaces and markets—who tend to children, the elderly, the planet, and so much more without financial compensation—are the bedrocks of community wealth. The work of financial activists includes making sure the value of their care labor is elevated, and that care workers never have to sacrifice themselves for the sake of others. There's enough for us all to thrive, together.

CONCLUSION
You Know a Lot

*As you get clearer about the future you are working
to create for yourself and the issues that you care about,
you start noticing opportunities and making decisions
today that will make that future possible.*

—TRISTA HARRIS, *Future Good*[1]

'll keep it brief. Why? Because you already know more than you'll need to be an effective financial activist.

I don't say that to brag about the completeness of this Playbook: on the contrary, I think the strategies, case studies, and tactics here are just an introduction for others to build upon. My confidence that you're ready to engage in financial activism comes from the fact that you've been an expert in your own lived experience *before* you even picked up this book.

Whether as passing thoughts or endless inquiry—experienced first-hand or witnessed from a seeming distance—you've known something was amiss with our financial systems for a while. You've likely had the nagging feeling that people deserve less poverty and more opportunities. That there is an alternative beyond just accepting that the world is burning or pretending everything is fine. That money can be a deep well of peace rather than a tidal wave of stress.

My hope for you is to never fall into the perfectionist trap that you're not "equipped" unless you have all the latest statistics or asset classes or [insert jargon here] memorized. This Playbook is your grounding tool to return to, scribble in, pass around, and flip through whenever you come across opportunities to influence money in line with personal and collective wealth building and well-being. And you *will* come across opportunities to influence money, potentially daily, especially when you're attuned to what to look for.

I hope you put this Playbook down knowing that I'm here for the long game: rooting you on in the work of reclaiming wealth and redirecting the flow of money—whether it's a few bucks or a few billion—wherever you are. My role is to support our collective agency, and you can help me lean into that work when you let me know about your experiences with financial activism. What strategies are you finding meaningful? What questions keep coming up? What infrastructure do we need to resource and build today, so we can all thrive a little bit more tomorrow?

Drop me a line through the submission form at *JasmineRashid.com*. Here you'll also find additional resources (like a **GLOSSARY OF ALL CAP-ITALIZED TERMS**), recommendations, and financial activist happenings I think you should know about that go beyond the limitations of this book.

As our collective ancestor Octavia Butler has gifted us: "The only lasting truth is change."[2] Thank you for remembering your claim to shape that change—in our economy, financial system, and beyond.

THE FINANCIAL ACTIVIST PLAYBOOK
DISCUSSION GUIDE

This discussion guide includes eighty questions—for your study group, strategy meeting, book club, or gathering—crafted with love.

the five-part pattern

Five key steps to becoming a financial activist, as demonstrated by interviewees of this Playbook

Chapter 4

1. Question: "Why is this like this?"

   a. Why do you think talking about money isn't more normalized in our culture?

   b. When was the last time you were in a discussion about the financial system? What was that like?

2. **Check-in: "How do I feel about this?"**

   a. Do you feel like you fully understand and appreciate your own money story?

   b. What tends to come up for you in conversations about our economic and financial systems? Do you experience confidence or uncertainty? Do you find it interesting or boring?

3. **Map: "What's possible?"**

   a. What potential benefits could you imagine if talking about money was less taboo among your family, friends, and community?

   b. What most excites you about a world where money as a topic is more transparent and trauma-informed?

4. **Ask yourself: "What can I do right now?"**

   a. Is there room for you to take better inventory of your personal finances, and know "what you're working with"?

   b. Who in your life would you most like to call and have an honest conversation about money with?

5. **Ask your community: "What can we do together?"**

   a. Imagine a gathering where everyone feels supported and well resourced to share their money stories and wealth-building goals. What makes the space supportive?

   b. What movement focus areas (e.g., tackling climate change, ending the racial and gender wealth gaps, increasing access to life-saving prescription drugs) do you think could benefit from more conversation and transparency around finance by everyday people?

Chapter 5

1. **Question: "Why is this like this?"**

   a. What, if anything, do you find confusing about banking?

   b. What is the reputation of banking institutions in your community?

2. Check-in: "How do I feel about this?"

   a. How do you feel about the bank(s) where you currently have a savings and/or checking account?

   b. Have you ever thought about what your savings are "up to" when they're in the bank, and what they're potentially helping fund?

3. Map: "What's possible?"

   a. What might happen if banks were accountable to communities instead of profit-seeking shareholders?

   b. Imagine your ideal bank. What types of personal perks and social/environmental benefits does it offer?

4. Ask yourself: "What can I do right now?"

   a. How might you find out if your bank is doing business with harmful industries and practices?

   b. Are there alternative options to big banks (community banks, credit unions, etc.) that you'd be interested in learning more about and opening an account at? Why?

5. Ask your community: "What can we do together?"

   a. For those who can't access traditional banks, how do we stop predatory lenders from taking advantage of them?

   b. What would it take to open a public bank in our region? Who would that benefit?

Chapter 6

1. Question: "Why is this like this?"

   a. What are some companies you find yourself feeling suspicious of? Why do you think that is?

   b. What comes to mind when you think of "conscious consumerism"?

2. **Check-in: "How do I feel about this?"**

   a. Think about the goods and services you've bought in the last week. What's the first word that comes to mind?

   b. Are there any goods or services you didn't feel great about buying but also didn't feel like you had many other options?

3. **Map: "What's possible?"**

   a. What would it realistically take for you to shop at local small businesses more regularly?

   b. What types of businesses can we leave behind in the outdated, extractive economy as we move into the next, regenerative economy?

4. **Ask yourself: "What can I do right now?"**

   a. Treat yourself! What values-aligned business in your community are you heading to? What are you buying? Why do you feel good about supporting them?

   b. How might you evaluate whether a new product or service is helping or harming community well-being and wealth building?

5. **Ask your community: "What can we do together?"**

   a. How might people in your community save money and reduce waste by sharing goods and services? Is this already happening in any capacity?

   b. What do you imagine are the most effective tactics that everyday people can use to influence companies to do better for people and the planet?

Chapter 7

1. **Question: "Why is this like this?"**

   a. Where do you think the majority of philanthropic money comes from?

b. Where does philanthropy show up in your community, and where is it clearly absent?

2. **Check-in: "How do I feel about this?"**

   a. Think about an experience where you benefited from a significant financial donation or gift. What do you feel in remembering that experience?

   b. Think about an experience where you made a significant financial donation or gift. What do you feel in remembering that experience?

3. **Map: "What's possible?"**

   a. What kind of philanthropist do you want your great-great-grandkids to remember you as?

   b. What are some ways that we can challenge the traditional power dynamic between those who donate and those who receive donations so that we're not reinforcing harmful "saviorism"?

4. **Ask yourself: "What can I do right now?"**

   a. Make a plan: if you were to find yourself in a financial crisis, what existing relationships would you lean on for support?

   b. Guesstimate what percentage of your income you donate to others on an annual basis. What would it take for you to increase that amount by 1 percent?

5. **Ask your community: "What can we do together?"**

   a. Imagine we're starting a giving circle. Who's in the circle, and what types of initiatives are we excited to collectively fundraise for and donate to?

   b. Are there ways for everyday people to make giving and receiving financial support more effective in your local community?

Chapter 8

1. Question: "Why is this like this?"

   a. Why do you think money is often seen as the most powerful form of capital?

   b. Throughout history to the present day, there have been efforts to stop and criminalize mutual aid efforts. What might be behind that?

2. Check-in: "How do I feel about this?"

   a. Can you recall a time when your community supported you beyond financial capital? If so, what was that experience like?

   b. Does the idea of participating in mutual aid intimidate you or comfort you? Why might that be?

3. Map: "What's possible?"

   a. What types of capital outside of financial capital do you think we might be undervaluing?

   b. How might mutual aid efforts in times of crisis not only help build back communities but also make them more resilient?

4. Ask yourself: "What can I do right now?"

   a. What are some self-care practices you can lean on more regularly and that could also benefit those around you?

   b. What's a nonfinancial offer, skill, and gift of yours that you find yourself excited to share with others?

5. Ask your community: "What can we do together?"

   a. What are some collective care practices our movements and organizations can lean on more regularly?

   b. Where and when might hosting an Offers and Needs Market be feasible and valuable? Who would come? How would you invite them?

Chapter 9

1. Question: "Why is this like this?"

    a. What does "budgets are a reflection of values" mean to you?

    b. Why don't everyday people have more of a say over how our tax dollars are spent?

2. Check-in: "How do I feel about this?"

    a. How might you know you're operating in the "enough" zone between your financial activity (spending, saving, investing, and redistributing) and your well-being?

    b. If you had to guess, what percentages of your income are spent on needs, reasonable wants, and unreasonable wants?

3. Map: "What's possible?"

    a. If everyday people in your town or city had a direct say over the local budget, what do you think would change? What services and infrastructure might improve?

    b. What might be possible if everyone received a guaranteed income to factor into their budgets?

4. Ask yourself: "What can I do right now?"

    a. What's an easy personal budgeting practice or tweak you can commit to so that budgeting feels empowering rather than draining?

    b. How might you positively influence the budget of an institution or organization you're connected to?

5. Ask your community: "What can we do together?"

    a. How can we implement participatory budgeting in our organization, institution, or community?

    b. What benefits might we see if there was collective debt cancellation? How can we contribute to existing organizing?

Chapter 10

1. **Question: "Why is this like this?"**

   a. Why might the concept of investing be intimidating or confusing to the everyday person?

   b. Why are women and people of color so drastically underrepresented among both the professional investment sector and those who receive investments?

2. **Check-in: "How do I feel about this?"**

   a. In one sentence, how would you describe your relationship to investing?

   b. Take stock of all the investments you currently have. How do you feel about them?

3. **Map: "What's possible?"**

   a. How can investing move money off Wall Street and into Main Street? Who would that benefit?

   b. What would it look like if everyday people had more opportunities to invest in businesses that align with their values?

4. **Ask yourself: "What can I do right now?"**

   a. If you have a retirement account, how might you figure out what you're actually invested in?

   b. What are some goals you have around investing? What's one thing you can do this week to get closer to those goals?

5. **Ask your community: "What can we do together?"**

   a. Are there existing opportunities to collectively invest in community enterprises that are building collective wealth and well-being?

   b. Are there opportunities for everyday people to partner with corporate shareholders to influence a company's policies and practices for the better?

Chapter 11

1. Question: "Why is this like this?"

   a. Why is workplace burnout such a common trend?

   b. Why might the concept of "being your own boss" resonate with so many people?

2. Check-in: "How do I feel about this?"

   a. How would you describe your relationship to work in the past and present?

   b. What kinds of work do you think are undervalued (and undercompensated) in our society?

3. Map: "What's possible?"

   a. If your bills were taken care of, how would you spend your days?

   b. How might a business be different if workers owned the business?

4. Ask yourself: "What can I do right now?"

   a. How might you realistically experiment with the "right to design" in your current workplace?

   b. Do you know of any employee-owned businesses that you'd be excited to support this week?

5. Ask your community: "What can we do together?"

   a. How can we support worker rights and union efforts en masse?

   b. What are the types of healthy business practices and norms we want to uplift in the next economy we're building?

BONUS

As a group, what's **one** act of financial activism that you can commit to today?

NOTES

Introduction

1. *Encyclopaedia Britannica*, "Alice Walker," Britannica's 100Women, August 18, 2020, *https://www.britannica.com/explore/100women/profiles/alice-walker*.

2. Kristalina Georgieva, "The Financial Sector in the 2020s: Building a More Inclusive System in the New Decade," International Monetary Fund, January 17, 2020, *https://www.imf.org/en/News/Articles/2020/01/17/sp01172019-the-financial-sector-in-the-2020s*.

3. Laura Rodini, "What Is the Great Wealth Transfer? When Does It Happen?" *The Street*, June 20, 2023, *https://www.thestreet.com/dictionary/g/great-wealth-transfer*.

4. Akaya Windwood in conversation with Rajasvini Bhansali for the Just Economy Institute, October 26, 2022.

Chapter 1

1. Deb Nelson, "Financial Activists Shift the Flow of Capital," SOCAP Global, November 21, 2019, *https://socapglobal.com/2019/11/financial-activists-shift-the-flow-of-capital/*.

2. Jason Lemon, "Majority of Gen Z Americans Hold Negative Views of Capitalism: Poll," *Newsweek*, June 25, 2021, *https://www.newsweek.com/majority-gen-z-americans-hold-negative-views-capitalism-poll-1604334*.

3. Clyde Haberman, "For Private Prisons, Detaining Immigrants Is Big Business," *New York Times*, October 1, 2018, *https://www.nytimes.com/2018/10/01/us/prisons-immigration-detention.html*.

4. Joe, "Lockup Quotas," In the Public Interest, October 11, 2013, *https://inthepublicinterest.org/lockup-quotas/*.

5. John Burnett, "Big Money as Private Immigrant Jails Boom," NPR, November 21, 2017, *https://www.npr.org/2017/11/21/565318778/big-money-as-private-immigrant-jails-boom*.

6. Rebecca Richard, "Dead to REITs: An Examination of the Rise and Fall of Private Prisons Financed through REITs," Georgetown Journal on Poverty

Law & Policy, November 3, 2022, *https://www.law.georgetown.edu/poverty-journal /blog/dead-to-reits-an-examination-of-the-rise-and-fall-of-private-prisons-financed -through-reits/.*

7. Molly Gott, "Who Is Profiting from Incarcerating Immigrant Families?," Eyes on the Ties, June 21, 2018, *https://news.littlesis.org/2018/06/21/who-is-profiting -from-incarcerating-immigrant-families/.*

8. Hand in Hand, "Wells & Chase: Break Up with Private Prisons!" (petition), Action Network, January 2019, *https://actionnetwork.org/petitions/wells-chase -break-up-with-private-prisons.*

9. Sue Udry, "#familiesbelongtogether Coalition Celebrates Valentine's Day at Wells Fargo and JP Morgan Chase Bank Branches Telling Big Banks to Break Up with Private Prisons," Defending Rights & Dissent, February 15, 2019, *https://www.rightsanddissent.org/news/familiesbelongtogether-coalition-celebrates -valentines-day-at-wells-fargo-and-jp-morgan-chase-bank-branches-telling-big-banks -to-break-up-with-private-prisons/.*

10. Brendan Krisel, "Protesters, Mariachis Rally Outside Chase CEO Jamie Dimon's Home," NY Patch, February 14, 2019, *https://patch.com/new-york/upper -east-side-nyc/protesters-mariachis-rally-outside-jamie-dimons-ues-home.*

11. Morgan Simon, "PNC Bank Pulls Out of the Private Prison Industry," *Forbes,* October 3, 2019, *https://www.forbes.com/sites/morgansimon/2019/08/09/pnc-bank -pulls-out-of-the-private-prison-industry/.*

12. John Adams, Claire Williams, Catherine Leffert, Jordan Stutts, and Allissa Kline, "JPMorgan Ends Financing of Private Prisons after Criticism," *American Banker,* June 1, 2021, *https://www.americanbanker.com/articles/jpmorgan-ends -financing-of-private-prisons-after-criticism.*

13. David Dayen, "The Private Prison Divestment Movement Just Had an Incredible Week," In These Times, March 14, 2019, *https://inthesetimes.com /article/private-prison-divestment-jpmorgan-ocasio-cortez-wells-fargo.*

14. Kathleen Joyce, "Bank of America to Stop Financing Private Prisons, Detention Centers," Fox Business, June 27, 2019, *https://www.foxbusiness.com/business -leaders/bank-of-america-announces-it-will-stop-financing-private-prisons-detention -centers.*

15. Imani Moise, "SunTrust to Stop Financing Private U.S. Prison Operators," Reuters, July 8, 2019, *https://www.reuters.com/article/idUSKCN1U31WU/;* Imani Moise, "BNP Paribas Backs Away from US Private Prison Industry," Reuters, July 13, 2019, *https://www.reuters.com/article/idUSKCN1U800S/;* Lananh Nguyen, "FITB Halts Financing to Private-Prison Firms." Bloomberg.com,

July 15, 2019. *https://www.bloomberg.com/news/articles/2019-07-15/fifth-third-to-halt-future-financing-to-private-prison-firms*; Dan Ennis, "Barclays Drops Its Role as Lead Underwriter in Prison Bond Sale," Banking Dive, April 16, 2021, *https://www.bankingdive.com/news/barclays-drops-its-role-as-lead-underwriter-in-prison-bond-sale/598556/*; Ryan Deto, "PNC Bank Will No Longer Finance the Private-Prison Industry," *Pittsburgh City Paper*, August 12, 2019, *https://www.pghcitypaper.com/news/pnc-bank-will-no-longer-finance-the-private-prison-industry-15596620*.

16. Dymond Green and Tala Hadavi, "Why Big Banks Could Be Killing Private Prisons," CNBC, January 2, 2020, *https://www.cnbc.com/2020/01/02/why-private-prisons-geo-group-and-corecivic-are-struggling-under-trump.html*.

17. Paul Verney, "US Private Prison Firm Hit by Rare ESG-Related Credit Downgrade Slams 'Virtue Signalling,'" Responsible Investor, August 9, 2019, *https://www.responsible-investor.com/corecivic-ratings/*.

18. Medha Chidambaram, Sytonia Reid, and Eleanor Greene, "Big Banks Leaving the Private Prison Business," Green America, n.d., *https://www.greenamerica.org/unraveling-fashion-industry/big-banks-leaving-private-prison-business*.

19. Jamie Birt, "25 Most Common Jobs in America," Indeed, March 10, 2023, *https://www.indeed.com/career-advice/finding-a-job/most-common-jobs-in-america*.

20. Stef W. Kight, "Chart: The Most Common Jobs, by Age and Pay," Axios, May 8, 2019, *https://www.axios.com/2019/05/08/common-jobs-age-pay-salary-millennials-careers*.

21. Tejas Vemparala, "Why Millennials and Gen Z Change Jobs Often," Business News Daily, n.d. *https://www.businessnewsdaily.com/7012-millennial-job-hopping.html*.

22. Deepa Iyer, "Social Change Ecosystem Map," Building Movement, January 26, 2023, *https://buildingmovement.org/our-work/movement-building/social-change-ecosystem-map/*.

23. Sasheen Andregg, interview with author, April 12, 2023.

24. Sophia Bollag, Elena Kadvany, Nora Mishanec, and Jessica Flores, "'Living in Shipping Containers': Half Moon Bay Shooting Reveals Poor Conditions on California Farms," *San Francisco Chronicle*, January 26, 2023, *https://www.sfchronicle.com/politics/article/living-in-shipping-containers-making-9-an-17742337.php*.

25. Anita Chabria, "Column: Shooting Uncovers 'Plantation Mentality' in a Rich, Liberal California Enclave," *Los Angeles Times*, February 9, 2023, *https://www.latimes.com/california/story/2023-02-09/column-after-shooting-farmworkers-fight-to-keep-our-attention-on-housing*.

26. Nwamaka Agbo, "What Is Restorative Economics?," n.d., *https://www
.nwamakaagbo.com/restorative-economics*.

27. Ali Berlow, *The Food Activist Handbook: Big & Small Things You Can Do to Help
Provide Fresh, Healthy Food for Your Community* (North Adams, MA: Capricorn
Link, 2015).

Chapter 2

1. Polina Peg, "Moving Together toward Liberation," Medium, July 8, 2020,
https://bthechange.com/moving-together-toward-liberation-f7bc04cea9ac.

2. Anita Tang, "Power Mapping and Analysis," The Commons: Social Change
Library, n.d., *https://commonslibrary.org/guide-power-mapping-and-analysis/*.

3. Cedric J. Robinson and Quan H L T, *Cedric J. Robinson: On Racial Capitalism,
Black Internationalism, and Cultures of Resistance* (London: Pluto Press, 2019.)

4. "Just Transition," Movement Generation, n.d., *https://movementgeneration.org
/justtransition/*.

5. "Explore the Eight Principles of a Regenerative Economy," Capital Institute,
August 14, 2023, *https://capitalinstitute.org/8-principles-regenerative-economy/*.

6. Shana Lebowitz and Marguerite Ward, "Here's How the 5-Day Workweek
Became So Popular in the First Place," *Business Insider*, February 1, 2023,
https://www.businessinsider.com/history-of-the-40-hour-workweek-2015-10.

7. Micah White, "The Master's Tools: The Wisdom of Audre Lorde," Activist
School, n.d., *https://www.activistgraduateschool.org/on-the-masters-tools*.

8. Barnard Center for Research on Women, "N'Tanya Lee: Building REAL Coa-
litional Queer Struggle," YouTube, June 26, 2019, *https://www.youtube.com
/watch?v=gg43uw_N2EQ*.

9. Bess Levin, "Mackenzie Scott Once Again Reminds People Jeff Bezos Is a
Cheapskate by Comparison," *Vanity Fair*, February 3, 2022, *https://www
.vanityfair.com/news/2022/02/mackenzie-scott-jeff-bezos-charitable-giving*.

10. Edgar Villanueva, *Decolonizing Wealth* (Oakland, CA: Berrett-Koehler Publishers, 2018).

11. Dasha Kennedy, "Money Musings: Become a Financial Activist," Fiscal
Femme, February 26, 2021, *https://thefiscalfemme.com/money-musings-posts
/become-financial-activist*.

12. Nick Hanauer, "The Top 1% of Americans Have Taken $50 Trillion from the
Bottom 90%—and That's Made the U.S. Less Secure," *TIME*, September 14,
2021, *https://time.com/5888024/50-trillion-income-inequality-america/*.

13. Mona Chalabi, "9 Ways to Imagine Jeff Bezos' Wealth," *New York Times*, April 7, 2022, *https://www.nytimes.com/interactive/2022/04/07/magazine/jeff-bezos-net-worth.html*.

14. Khanyi Mlaba, "The Richest 1% Own Almost Half the World's Wealth & 9 Other Mind-Blowing Facts on Wealth Inequality," Global Citizen, January 19, 2023, *https://www.globalcitizen.org/en/content/wealth-inequality-oxfam -billionaires-elon-musk/#:~:text=The%20richest%201%25%20own%20almost %20half%20of%20the%20world's%20wealth,99%25%20of%20the%20world's %20population*.

15. Anonymous contributors and Sierra Club staff, "Radical Means Grabbing Something by the Root," Sierra Club, June 16, 2020, *https://www.sierraclub.org /texas/blog/2020/06/radical-means-grabbing-something-root#:~:text=Angela%20 Davis%2C%20a%20trail%2Dblazing,largest%20being%20modern%2Dday%20 policing*.

Chapter 3

1. Joseph E. Stiglitz, *The Price of Inequality: How Today's Divided Society Endangers Our Future* (New York: W.W. Norton, 2013).

2. Lisa Camner McKay, "How the Racial Wealth Gap Has Evolved—and Why It Persists," Federal Reserve Bank of Minneapolis, October 3, 2022, *https://www .minneapolisfed.org/article/2022/how-the-racial-wealth-gap-has-evolved-and-why-it -persists#:~:text=While%20the%20White%2DBlack%20income,shows%20no %20sign%20of%20resolving*.

3. Tracy Jan, "1 in 7 White Families Are Now Millionaires. For Black Families, It's 1 in 50," *Washington Post*, November 24, 2021, *https://www.washingtonpost .com/news/wonk/wp/2017/10/03/white-families-are-twice-as-likely-to-be-millionaires -as-a-generation-ago/*.

4. "To What Extent Was Our Economy Designed to Be Fair?," Take On Wall Street, April 9, 2021, *https://isoureconomyfair.org/*.

5. Marjorie Kelly, *Wealth Supremacy: How the Extractive Economy and the Biased Rules of Capitalism Drive Today's Crises* (Oakland, CA: Berrett-Koehler Publishers, 2023).

6. Josh Bivens and Jori Kandra, "CEO Pay Has Skyrocketed 1,460% since 1978," Economic Policy Institute, October 4, 2022, *https://www.epi.org /publication/ceo-pay-in-2021/*.

7. Josh Bivens, Elize Gould, and Lawrence Mishel, "Wage Stagnation in Nine Charts," Economic Policy Institute, January 6, 2015, *https://www.epi.org /publication/charting-wage-stagnation/*.

8. Bivens, Gould, and Mishel, "Wage Stagnation."
9. "Just Transition: A Framework for Change," Climate Justice Alliance, March 15, 2023, *https://climatejusticealliance.org/just-transition/*.
10. Barry Schwartz, *The Paradox of Choice: Why More Is Less* (New York: Ecco, 2016).
11. United Frontline Table, *A People's Orientation to a Regenerative Economy* (Oakland, CA: Climate Justice Alliance, 2022), *https://climatejusticealliance.org /regenerativeeconomy/#:~:text=A%20People's%20Orientation%20to%20a%20 Regenerative%20Economy%20offers%20community%20groups,for%20frontline%20 communities%20and%20workers*.
12. "The Solidarity Economy," New Economy Coalition, March 6, 2023, *https:// neweconomy.net/solidarity-economy/#:~:text=A%20solidarity%20economy%20 ecosystem%20is,healthcare%20and%20healing%2C%20and%20transportation*.
13. "What is Biomimicry?," Biomimicry Institute, n.d., *https://biomimicry.org /what-is-biomimicry/*.
14. Robin Wall Kimmerer, *Braiding Sweetgrass* (Minneapolis: Milkweed Editions, 2013).
15. Tema Okun, "White Supremacy Culture," n.d., *https://www.whitesupremacyculture.info/*.
16. adrienne maree brown, *Emergent Strategy: Shaping Change, Changing Worlds* (Chico, CA: AK Press, 2021).

Chapter 4

1. Gabe Dunn, *Bad with Money: The Imperfect Art of Getting Your Financial Sh*t Together* (New York: Atria Books, 2019).
2. Empower, "Money Talks," The Currency, January 10, 2023, *https://www.empower .com/the-currency/money/money-talks*.
3. Nafasi Ferrell, interview with the author, May 22, 2023.
4. "Race, Finance, Equity: Narratives Unbound," Narratives Unbound, n.d., *https:// www.narrativesunbound.net/*.
5. Empower, "Money Talks."
6. Chantel Chapman, interview with the author, April 16, 2023.
7. "Trauma of Money," n.d., *https://www.thetraumaofmoney.com/*.
8. Sara Murphy, "What Is Financial Trauma?," Shondaland, September 15, 2023, *https://www.shondaland.com/live/money/a45103549/what-is-financial-trauma/*.
9. Chantel Chapman, "The Trauma of Money with Chantel Chapman," interview by Paco De Leon, Hell Yeah Group, April 2, 2023, *https://thehellyeahgroup .com/the-weird-finance-podcast/weird-finance-s1e7*.

10. Delia O'Hara, "Brad Klontz Is Concerned with How Experiences Affect Our Relationship with Money," American Psychological Association, January 19, 2023, https://www.apa.org/members/content/money-relationship.

11. Dr. Brad Klontz, "Klontz Money Script® Inventory-Revised (KMSI-R)," BradKlontz.com, n.d., https://www.bradklontz.com/moneyscriptstest.

12. "Class Privilege Quiz," Resource Generation, August 25, 2020, https://resourcegeneration.org/start-your-journey/quiz/.

13. Esther Park, interview with the author, July 18, 2023.

14. Berna Anat, Money Out Loud: All the Financial Stuff No One Taught Us (New York: Quill Tree Books, 2023).

Chapter 5

1. Mehrsa Baradaran, The Color of Money: Black Banks and the Racial Wealth Gap (Cambridge, MA: The Belknap Press of Harvard University Press, 2017).

2. Stephone Coward II, interview with the author, January 11, 2022.

3. Karen Bennett, "What Are Black-Owned Banks and How Do You Support Them?," Bankrate, February 20, 2023, https://www.bankrate.com/banking/how-to-support-black-owned-banks/.

4. Fast Company Staff, "The Best Graphic Design of 2022," Fast Company, September 15, 2022, https://www.fastcompany.com/90771066/graphic-design-innovation-by-design-2022.

5. Board of Governors of the Federal Reserve System, "Banking and Credit," Federal Reserve, May 2019, https://www.federalreserve.gov/publications/2019-economic-well-being-of-us-households-in-2018-banking-and-credit.htm.

6. Chi Chi Wong, "Overdraft Fees: From Perk to Penalty," interview by Adrian Me and Stacey Vanek Smith, The Indicator from Planet Money podcast, NPR, January 24, 2022, https://www.npr.org/2022/01/20/1074521609/overdraft-fees-from-perk-to-penalty.

7. Megan Leonhardt, "Why This Bank Exec's Boat Name Is Now Part of a Federal Lawsuit," Money, January 17, 2017, https://money.com/tcf-bank-ceo-boat-overdraft-lawsuit/.

8. Baradaran, The Color of Money.

9. Manoj Singh, "The 2007–2008 Financial Crisis in Review," Investopedia, March 19, 2023, https://www.investopedia.com/articles/economics/09/financial-crisis-review.asp.

10. Brian Kreiswirth and Anna-Marie Tabor, "What You Need to Know about the Equal Credit Opportunity Act and How It Can Help You," Consumer

Financial Protection Bureau, October 31, 2016, *https://www.consumerfinance .gov/about-us/blog/what-you-need-know-about-equal-credit-opportunity-act-and-how -it-can-help-you-why-it-was-passed-and-what-it/*; Deborah Sweeney, "How HR 5050 Changed Entrepreneurship for Women," *Forbes*, August 21, 2018, *https:// www.forbes.com/sites/deborahsweeney/2018/08/21/how-hr-5050-changed -entrepreneurship-for-women/?sh=72f3b24911a5*.

11. Robert Bartlett, Adair Morse, Richard Stanton, and Nancy Wallace, "Consumer-Lending Discrimination in the FinTech Era," *Journal of Financial Economics* 143, no. 1 (2022): 30–56, *https://doi.org/10.1016/j.jfineco.2021.05.047*.

12. Price Fishback, Jessica LaVoice, Allison Shertzer, and Randall Walsh, "The HOLC Maps: How Race and Poverty Influenced Real Estate Professionals' Evaluation of Lending Risk in the 1930s," *Journal of Economic History* 83, no. 4 (2023): 1019–56, *https://doi.org/10.1017/S0022050723000475*.

13. Ann Choi, Bill Dedman, Keith Herbert, and Olivia Winslow, "Long Island Divided," *Newsday*, November 17, 2017, *https://projects.newsday.com/long-island /real-estate-agents-investigation/*.

14. "Attorney General James Stops Discriminatory Practices at Long Island Real Estate Brokerage," press release, Office of the New York State Attorney General, March 15, 2023, *https://ag.ny.gov/press-release/2023/attorney-general -james-stops-discriminatory-practices-long-island-real-estate*.

15. "Small Business Lending by Size of Institution, 2018," Institute for Local Self-Reliance, May 14, 2019, *https://ilsr.org/small-business-lending-by-size -of-institution-2014/*.

16. Evelyn Holmes, "Alpha Kappa Alpha Sorority Opens FMO Credit Union, First of Its Kind in American History," ABC7 Chicago, July 13, 2023, *https:// abc7chicago.com/aka-sorority-alpha-kapa-credit-union-fmo/13495073/*.

17. Oscar Perry Abello, "This Black Barber Opened the First Credit Union in Arkansas since 1996," Next City, February 7, 2023, *https://nextcity.org/urbanist -news/this-black-barber-opened-the-first-credit-union-in-arkansas-since-1996*.

18. "About Us," Beneficial State Bank, n.d., *https://www.beneficialstatebank.com /about-us*.

19. Caitlin Duffy, interview with the author, April 5, 2023.

20. "Our Story," Amalgamated Bank, n.d., *https://amalgamatedbank.com/our-story*.

21. Ariel Brooks, Libbie Cohn, and Aaron Tanaka, "Social Movement Investing," Center for Economic Democracy, *https://dd3393f7-04d7-4015-80f3-f7f9 ca94f8ee.filesusr.com/ugd/40c717_a9b518bcab8348e9a38a85dd99f217c1.pdf*.

22. Deonna Anderson, "Standing Rock's Surprising Legacy: A Push for Public Banks," *YES!* magazine, July 28, 2022, *https://www.yesmagazine.org/issue/good -money/2019/01/02/standing-rocks-surprising-legacy-a-push-for-public-banks.*

23. "Key Findings," First Peoples Worldwide, April 25, 2019, *https://www.colorado .edu/program/fpw/DAPL-case-study.*

24. Board of Governors of the Federal Reserve System, "Banking and Credit."

25. Jasmine Rashid, "I'm committing to opening up a new account at a mission-aligned financial institution by the end of the week. Drop your favorite #creditunion or non-trash #bank here! Thank you in advance! P.S. I'm in Oakland so local suggestions are very welcome." LinkedIn, March 20, 2023, *https://www.linkedin.com/posts/jasminerashid_creditunion-bank-crowdsourcing-activity -7044016713918529537-GrvH?originalSubdomain=rw.*

26. Self-Help Credit Union, n.d., *https://www.self-helpfcu.org/.*

27. "Public Banks: Bank of North Dakota," Institute for Local Self-Reliance, n.d., *https://ilsr.org/rule/bank-of-north-dakota-2/#:~:text=North%20Dakota%20is%20the %20only,assist%20in%20the%20development%20of%E2%80%A6.*

28. "Legislation by State," Public Banking Institute, n.d., *https://publicbankinginstitute .org/legislation-by-state/.*

29. "Community Benefit Agreements," California Reinvestment Coalition, n.d., *https://rise-economy.org/publications/bank-agreements/.*

30. Board of Governors of the Federal Reserve System, "Community Reinvestment Act (CRA)," Federal Reserve, August 24, 2022, *https://www.federalreserve .gov/consumerscommunities/cra_about.htm.*

Chapter 6

1. Gabor Maté and Daniel Maté, *The Myth of Normal: Trauma, Illness & Healing in a Toxic Culture* (New York: Avery, 2022).

2. Skyler Verrone, "Amazon Has a History of Mistreating Its Employees," The Triangle, January 11, 2019, *https://www.thetriangle.org/opinion/amazon-has-a-history -of-mistreating-its-employees/*; Olivier O'Connell, "Frustrated Worker's Email to Bezos May Change Way Amazon Pays Everyone," *The Independent,* October 27, 2021, *https://www.independent.co.uk/money/amazon-underpaying-workers-email-jeff -bezos-b1946473.html*; Noam Scheiber, "Judge Finds Amazon Broke Labor Law in Anti-union Effort," January 31, 2023, *https://www.nytimes.com/2023/01 /31/business/economy/amazon-union-staten-island-nlrb.html*; Matthew Gardner, "Amazon Avoids More than $5 Billion in Corporate Income Taxes, Reports 6 Percent Tax Rate on $35 Billion of US Income," Institute on Taxation and

Economic Policy, February 7, 2022, *https://itep.org/amazon-avoids-more-than-5 -billion-in-corporate-income-taxes-reports-6-percent-tax-rate-on-35-billion-of-us -income/*; Karen Hao, "Amazon Is the Invisible Backbone of ICE's Immigration Crackdown," *MIT Technology Review*, April 2, 2020, *https://www.technologyreview .com/2018/10/22/139639/amazon-is-the-invisible-backbone-behind-ices-immigration -crackdown/*; Vincent Manancourt, "Millions of People's Data Is at Risk"— Amazon Insiders Sound Alarm over Security," Politico, December 2, 2021, *https://www.politico.eu/article/data-at-risk-amazon-security-threat/*; Antara Haldar, "Opinion: Amazon's Business Model Is Inhumane and Unsustainable," MarketWatch, October 1, 2022, *https://www.marketwatch.com/story/amazons -business-model-is-inhumane-and-unsustainable-11664560894*; Will Evans, "Private Report Shows How Amazon Drastically Undercounts Its Carbon Footprint," Reveal, February 25, 2022, *https://revealnews.org/article/private-report-shows -how-amazon-drastically-undercounts-its-carbon-footprint/*.

3. Melissa Daniels, "How Bookshop.org Used Prime Day to Court Anti-Amazon Shoppers," Modern Retail, July 17, 2023, *https://www.modernretail.co /marketing/how-bookshop-org-used-prime-day-to-court-anti-amazon-shoppers/*.

4. Office of the Assistant Secretary for Health (OASH), "New Surgeon General Advisory Raises Alarm about the Devastating Impact of the Epidemic of Loneliness and Isolation in the United States," HHS.gov, May 3, 2023, *https:// www.hhs.gov/about/news/2023/05/03/new-surgeon-general-advisory-raises-alarm -about-devastating-impact-epidemic-loneliness-isolation-united-states.html*.

5. Kate Knibbs, "How Bookshop.org Survives-and Thrives-in Amazon's World," *Wired*, April 11, 2023, *https://www.wired.com/story/books-bookshop-org-thrives -amazon-world/*.

6. Philipp Chmel, "You Can't Save the Planet by Yourself," *Jacobin*, September 24, 2019, *https://jacobin.com/2019/09/climate-crisis-ethical-consumption-greta -thunberg-environment*.

7. "New Report Shows Just 100 Companies Are Source of over 70% of Emissions," CDP, July 10, 2017, *https://www.cdp.net/en/articles/media/new-report-shows -just-100-companies-are-source-of-over-70-of-emissions*.

8. Joshua Karliner, "A Brief History of Greenwash," CorpWatch, March 22, 2001, *https://www.corpwatch.org/article/brief-history-greenwash*.

9. Andrew Nakamura, "The History of Greenwashing and Its Modern Evolution," September 25, 2022, *https://www.theclimateclub.co/sustainabilityblog/the -history-of-greenwashing-and-its-modern-evolution*.

10. Morgan Simon, "Aurora James Is Helping Companies Invest in Accountability with the '15 Percent Pledge,'" *Forbes*, December 21, 2020,

*https://www.forbes.com/sites/morgansimon/2020/12/21/aurora-james-is-helping
-companies-invest-in-accountability-with-the-15-percent-pledge/?sh=4f3098e17821.*

11. Liam Hess, "Aurora James on Her 15 Percent Pledge Campaign to Support Black-Owned Businesses," *Vogue*, June 6, 2020, *https://www.vogue.com/article /aurora-james-brother-vellies-15-percent-pledge-small-business-spotlight.*

12. Sara Li, "Aurora James Proposes '15 Percent Pledge' to Help Black Businesses Long-Term," *Teen Vogue*, June 4, 2020, *https://www.teenvogue.com/story/aurora -james-15-percent-pledge.*

13. "The Fifteen Percent Pledge," n.d., *https://15percentpledge.org/.*

14. "The Impact of Covid-19 on the People Who Make Our Clothes," Fashion Revolution, n.d., *https://www.fashionrevolution.org/covid19/.*

15. Jana Kasperkevic, "Rana Plaza Collapse: Workplace Dangers Persist Three Years Later, Reports Find," *Guardian*, May 31, 2016, *https://www.theguardian.com /business/2016/may/31/rana-plaza-bangladesh-collapse-fashion-working-conditions.*

16. Heather Snowden, "#PayUp: Two Years Later," Remake, March 30, 2022, *https://remake.world/stories/payup-two-years-later/.*

17. Charlese Banks, interview with the author, April 28, 2023.

18. Yusra Farzan, "How Tacos and the 'Pink Hijabi of Orange County' Are Bringing Latino and Muslim Communities Together," PBS SoCal, July 6, 2022, *https:// www.pbssocal.org/shows/the-migrant-kitchen/rida-hamida-taco-trucks-in-every-mosque.*

19. Gustavo Arellano, "Column: A COVID Vaccine with Your Tacos? Just a Day's Work for This Muslim Activist," *Los Angeles Times*, May 7, 2021, *https://www .latimes.com/california/story/2021-05-07/taco-trucks-at-every-mosque-rida-hamida.*

20. Caleigh Wells, "Want to Fight Climate Change and Food Waste? One App Can Do Both," NPR, October 3, 2023, *https://www.npr.org/2023/10/03 /1202278468/climate-change-food-waste-too-good-to-go.*

21. Andrew Thomas, "The Secret Ratio That Proves Why Customer Reviews Are So Important," Inc.com, February 6, 2018, *https://www.inc.com/andrew-thomas /the-hidden-ratio-that-could-make-or-break-your-company.html.*

22. "Boycott," Encyclopædia Britannica, n.d., *https://www.britannica.com/money/boycott.*

23. Lucas Frau, "Why Are People Boycotting Starbucks? A Look Inside the Scrutiny of the Coffee Chain," NorthJersey.com, December 14, 2023, *https://www .northjersey.com/story/news/nation/2023/12/14/starbucks-why-everyone-boycotting -controversies-explained/71885557007/.*

24. Jena McGregor, "Why 'Buycotts' Could Overtake Boycotts among Consumer Activists," *Washington Post*, February 28, 2018, *https://www.washingtonpost.com/news /on-leadership/wp/2018/02/28/why-buycotts-could-overtake-boycotts-among-consumer -activists/.*

25. Chaviva Gordon-Bennett, "Corporate Event Planning: Checklist and Guide," Bizzabo, June 26, 2023, *https://www.bizzabo.com/blog/corporate-event-planning -guide#:~:text=According%20to%20a%20report%20from,2030%2C%20growing %2017.3%25%20annually.*

Chapter 7

1. Edgar Villanueva, *Decolonizing Wealth* (Oakland, CA: Berrett-Koehler Publishers, 2018).

2. Rund Abdelfatah, Ramtin Arablouei, Julie Caine, Lawrence Wu, Laine Kaplan-Levenson, Victor Yvellez, and Casey Miner, "The New Gilded Age," *Throughline* podcast, NPR, December 29, 2022, *https://www.npr.org/2022 /04/26/1094794267/the-new-gilded-age.*

3. Anand Giridharadas, *Winners Take All: The Elite Charade of Changing the World* (New York: Alfred A. Knopf, 2018).

4. INCITE! Women of Color against Violence, *The Revolution Will Not Be Funded: Beyond the Prison Industrial Complex* (Cambridge, MA: South End Press, 2007).

5. Lucy Bernholz, *How We Give Now: A Philanthropic Guide for the Rest of Us* (Cambridge, MA: MIT Press, 2023).

6. Desirae Calloway, interview with the author, July 18, 2023.

7. Dr. Kortney Ziegler, interview with the author, May 23, 2023.

8. Grace Bassekele, interview with the author, July 20, 2023.

9. Hella Heart Oakland Giving Circle, interview with the author, April 16, 2023.

Chapter 8

1. Daniel Fernandez, "Dean Spade on the Promise of Mutual Aid," The Nation, December 16, 2020, *https://www.thenation.com/article/economy/interview-dean -spade/.*

2. "Relationships Don't Have to Be Complicated," 5 Love Languages, n.d., *https://5lovelanguages.com/.*

3. Kelly Hayes and Mariame Kaba, *Let This Radicalize You: Organizing and the Revolution of Reciprocal Care* (Chicago: Haymarket Book, 2023).

4. "Free the Land Capital Campaign," Movement Generation, n.d., *https:// movementgeneration.org/freetheland/.*

5. Mia Sato, "Buy Nothing Exploded on Facebook—Now It Wants a Platform of Its Own," The Verge, June 12, 2022, *https://www.theverge.com/tech/2022/1/12 /22878353/buy-nothing-groups-facebook-app.*

6. Crystal Arnold, interview with the author, May 3, 2023.

Chapter 9

1. Womens Foundation California, "Top 5 Quotes from the California Budget Project's Conference on Public Policy," March 20, 2014, *https://womensfoundca .org/top-5-quotes-from-the-california-budget-projects-conference-on-public-policy/*.

2. Kory Taylor and Elizabeth B. Jones, "Adult Dehydration," *StatPearls* (2023), *https://www.ncbi.nlm.nih.gov/books/NBK555956/*.

3. Ariel and Nathaniel Brooks, interview with the author, August 30, 2023.

4. Jasmine Rashid, LinkedIn, August 2023, *https://www.linkedin.com/posts /jasminerashid_bipocsmallbusiness-oaklandcitycouncil-peoplepower-activity -7093275971629285376-12pR*.

5. The Intercept, "Your Debt Is Someone Else's Asset," YouTube, December 9, 2021, *https://www.youtube.com/watch?v=Bhn3jsBHKg4*.

6. Boston Ujima Project, "Aligning Pension Money with Community Values," Facebook post, February 27, 2019, *https://www.facebook.com/bostonujimaproject /posts/people-want-to-be-involved-in-the-investment-decision-making-process-we -need-dem/2156490961040302/*.

7. Brian Wampler and Mike Touchton, "Brazil Let Its Citizens Make Decisions about City Budgets. Here's What Happened," *Washington Post*, January 22, 2014, *https://www.washingtonpost.com/news/monkey-cage/wp/2014/01/22 /brazil-let-its-citizens-make-decisions-about-city-budgets-heres-what-happened/? noredirect=on*.

8. "Case Studies," Participatory Budgeting Project, n.d., *https://www.participatory budgeting.org/case-studies/*.

9. Celina Su, "Budgeting Justice," *Boston Review*, February 10, 2022, *https://www .bostonreview.net/articles/budgeting-justice/*.

10. Nashville People's Budget Coalition, "Demands for a Nashville People's Budget, 2021–2022," June 2021, *https://nashvillepeoplesbudget.files.wordpress.com /2021/06/npbc-demands-report-2021-1.pdf*.

11. Participatory Budgeting Project, "People's Budgets 101: From LA to Nashville" (webinar), Vimeo, August 27, 2023, *https://vimeo.com/849232743*.

12. "The Magnolia Mother's Trust," Springboard to Opportunities, n.d., *https:// springboardto.org/magnolia-mothers-trust/*.

13. Just Economy Institute, "Fireside Chat with Aisha Nyandoro, Springboard to Opportunities, and Donna Daniels, Heron Foundation," June 27, 2023.

14. Aisha Nyandoro, "What Does 'Wealth' Mean to You?," TED Talk, October 2023, *https://www.ted.com/talks/aisha_nyandoro_what_does_wealth_mean_to_you*.

15. Rachel Treisman, "California Program Giving $500 No-Strings-Attached Stipends Pays Off, Study Finds," NPR, March 4, 2021, *https://www.npr.org/2021/03/04/973653719/california-program-giving-500-no-strings-attached-stipends-pays-off-study-finds.*

16. Annie Thériault, "Richest 1% Bag Nearly Twice as Much Wealth as the Rest of the World Put Together over the Past Two Years," press release, Oxfam International, January 16, 2023, *https://www.oxfam.org/en/press-releases/richest-1-bag-nearly-twice-much-wealth-rest-world-put-together-over-past-two-years.*

Chapter 10

1. Rachel Rodgers, *We Should All Be Millionaires: A Woman's Guide to Earning More, Building Wealth, and Gaining Economic Power* (New York: HarperCollins, 2021).

2. Zoe Thomas, "The Hidden Links between Slavery and Wall Street," BBC News, August 29, 2019, *https://www.bbc.com/news/business-49476247.*

3. History.com Editors, "SEC: Securities and Exchange Commission," History.com, December 6, 2019, *https://www.history.com/topics/us-government-and-politics/securities-and-exchange-commission.*

4. TheStreet, "Why the NYSE Trading Floor Is a Lot Quieter These Days," YouTube, July 6, 2023, *https://www.youtube.com/watch?v=kZsG--9wm7s.*

5. Lorraine Boissoneault, "How the New York Stock Exchange Gave Abbie Hoffman His Start in Guerrilla Theater," *Smithsonian Magazine*, August 24, 2017, *https://www.smithsonianmag.com/history/how-new-york-stock-exchange-gave-abbie-hoffman-his-start-guerrilla-theater-180964612/.*

6. Matt Brannon, "State of Retirement Finances: 2023 Edition," Clever Real Estate, February 27, 2023, *https://listwithclever.com/research/retirement-finances-2023/#average-retirement-savings.*

7. Ellevest Team, "Explainer: How Does Employer 401(k) Matching Work?," Ellevest, October 14, 2022, *https://www.ellevest.com/magazine/retirement/401k-employer-match.*

8. *Money, Explained*, episode 5, "Retirement," featuring Marcia Gay Harden, Hal Hershfield, and Teresa Guilarducci, aired May 11, 2021, on Netflix.

9. "99% of 401(k) Plans Have No Climate-Friendly Option," Social(K) blog, June 22, 2023, *https://socialk.com/blog/atmosphere-99-of-401k-plans-have-no-climate-friendly-option/.*

10. US Securities and Exchange Commission, "About EDGAR," SEC Emblem, January 23, 2020. *https://www.sec.gov/edgar/about#:~:text=EDGAR%2C%20the%20Electronic%20Data%20Gathering,Investment%20Company%20Act%20of%201940.*

11. Rosemary Arriada-Keiper, "Celebrating Five Years of Global Gender Pay Parity at Adobe," Adobe Blog, March 14, 2023, *https://blog.adobe.com/en /publish/2023/03/14/celebrating-five-years-global-gender-pay-parity-at-adobe#: ~:text=In%202018%2C%20Adobe%20was%20one,of%20their%20gender %20or%20ethnicity.*

12. "NIAGX: Investing with Purpose," Nia Impact Capital, March 10, 2022, *https://niaimpactfunds.com/.*

13. Kristin Hull, interview with the author, October 9, 2023.

14. Zahra Hirji, "How to Purge Fossil Fuel Investments from Your 401(k) or IRA," Bloomberg, October 20, 2022, *https://www.bloomberg.com/news/features /2022-10-20/how-to-purge-fossil-fuel-investments-from-your-401-k-or-ira.*

15. Belinda Luscombe, "How Hedge Funds' Lack of Diversity Affects All of Us," *Time*, January 5, 2022, *https://time.com/6132594/hedged-out-book-hedge-fund -inequality/#:~:text=A%20recent%20Knight%20Foundation%20study,of%20the %20more%20diverse%20firms.*

16. Michael Iachini, "How Well Has Environmental, Social, and Governance Investing Performed?," Schwab Brokerage, September 19, 2021, *https://www .schwab.com/learn/story/how-well-has-environmental-social-and-governance-investing -performed#:~:text=The%20differences%20have%20tended%20to,comes%20to %20risk%20or%20returns.*

17. Aaran Fronda, "How to File (and Pass) a Resolution," ESG Investor, April 19, 2023, *https://www.esginvestor.net/how-to-file-and-pass-a-resolution/.*

18. "Empowering Shareholders to Change Corporations for Good," As You Sow, n.d., *https://www.asyousow.org/?gclid=CjwKCAjwp8OpBhAFEiwAG7NaEruLn2J _9bLnqSZYQbLCDydqCiaUzZm4QIzOeQZEPi0h-qU1tBRbvhoCyXYQAvD _BwE;* "Who We Are," Majority Action, n.d., *https://www.majorityaction.us/;* "How We Advance Justice," Corporate Accountability, n.d., *https://corporate accountability.org/?gclid=CjwKCAjwp8OpBhAFEiwAG7NaEhQoylbytdwMsQapt FdYLGEfZlu-0sYDDNd2lpTGRrpnt2MrRXrUhhoCVcEQAvD_BwE.*

19. "Action Center for Corporate Accountability," American Friends Service Committee, n.d., *https://afsc.org/programs/action-center-corporate-accountability;* Gregory Gethard, "Protest Divestment and the End of Apartheid," Investo- pedia, July 22, 2022, *https://www.investopedia.com/articles/economics/08/protest -divestment-south-africa.asp.*

20. May CI van Schalkwyk, Pascal Diethelm, and Martin McKee, "The Tobacco Industry Is Dying; Disinvestment Can Speed Its Demise," *European Journal of Public Health* 29, no. 4 (2019): 599–600, *https://doi.org/10.1093/eurpub/ckz006.*

21. "Wall Street Is Funding Climate Destruction," Stop the Money Pipeline, n.d., *https://stopthemoneypipeline.com/*.

22. "Investigate: Action/Research on State Violence," American Friends Service Committee, n.d., *https://investigate.afsc.org/*.

23. Adriana Abizadeh, interview with the author, May 25, 2023.

24. Justin Phillips, "A Bygone Jazz Club Is the Forgotten Story of Oakland's 'Harlem of the West' Era," *San Francisco Chronicle*, October 31, 2019, *https://www.sfchronicle.com/food/article/A-bygone-jazz-club-is-the-forgotten-story-of-14583167.php*.

25. Natalie Orenstein, "This Oakland Co-Op Wants to Revive the Legendary Esther's Orbit Room and the Seventh Street Corridor," The Oaklandside, June 9, 2021, *https://oaklandside.org/2021/06/09/this-oakland-co-op-wants-to-revive-the-legendary-esthers-orbit-room-and-the-seventh-street-corridor/*.

26. Michelle Tran Maryns, interview with the author, March 29, 2023.

27. "Jumpstart Our Business Startups (JOBS) Act," Fundrise, n.d., *https://fundrise.com/education/glossary/jumpstart-our-business-startups-jobs-act*.

28. Arno Hesse, interview with the author, June 2, 2023.

29. "Invest in Coco Noir Wine Shop & Bar." CoCo Noir Wine Shop & Bar, n.d. *https://wefunder.com/coconoirwineshop*.

30. Alicia Kidd talk for Slow Money and Food Funded event, May 19, 2023.

31. "Circle Experience," Invest for Better, n.d., *https://investforbetter.org/circles/*.

32. "About Matriarch Funds," Native Women Lead, n.d., *https://www.nativewomenlead.org/new-page-5*; Sara Shawanokasic, "The Future Is Indigenous Women," Native Forward Scholars Fund, November 2, 2021, *https://issuu.com/AmericanIndianGraduateCenter/docs/fall_2021_aigc_pdfs/13862277*.

33. leo freeman, interview with the author, October 12, 2023.

Chapter 11

1. National Portrait Gallery, "Living Self-Portrait: Dolores Huerta - National Portrait Gallery," YouTube, October 5, 2015, *https://youtu.be/PDgBPT5cEhQ?si=7fhat-ElF1ZwOGsb*.

2. Sarah Jaffe, *Work Won't Love You Back: How Devotion to Our Jobs Keeps Us Exploited, Exhausted, and Alone* (London: Hurst, 2022).

3. Naima McQueen, interview with the author, September 14, 2023.

4. "Entrepreneur Statistics," ThinkImpact.com, July 20, 2022, *https://www.thinkimpact.com/entrepreneur-statistics/*.

5. Jess Rimington and Joanna L. Cea, *Beloved Economies: Transforming How We Work* (Vancouver, BC: Page Two, 2022).

6. "Union Facts: The Value of Collective Voice: AFL-CIO," AFL, n.d., *https://aflcio
.org/formaunion/collective-voice*.

7. Nicole Fortin, Thomas Lemieux, and Neil Lloyd, "Impacts of Right-to-Work
Laws on Unionization and Wages," Summary of NBER Working Paper
30098, NBER *Digest*, November 8, 2022, *https://www.nber.org/digest/202208
/impacts-right-work-laws-unionization-and-wages*.

8. Steven Greenhouse, "'The Success Is Inspirational': The Fight for $15 Move-
ment 10 Years On," *The Guardian*, November 23, 2022, *https://www.theguardian
.com/us-news/2022/nov/23/fight-for-15-movement-10-years-old*.

9. "UTLA Members Win Ground-Breaking Tentative Agreement," UTLA,
April 18, 2023, *https://utla.net/utla-members-win-ground-breaking-tentative-agreement/*.

10. Jason Del Rey, "America Finally Gets an Amazon Union," Vox, April 1, 2022,
https://www.vox.com/recode/23005336/amazon-union-new-york-warehouse.

11. Yoni Hirshberg, Megan Cassingham, and Sara Wexler, "Graduate Student
Workers at the University of Southern California Have Won a Union,"
Jacobin, May 3, 2023, *https://jacobin.com/2023/03/university-of-southern-california
-grad-student-workers-union-bargaining-demands-nlrb*; JC Tretter, "NFL Econom-
ics 101," NFL Players Association, October 27, 2021, *https://nflpa.com/posts/nfl
-economics-101*; Marilyn Bechtel, "San Francisco Marriott Workers Celebrate
New Contract," People's World, December 6, 2018, *https://www.peoplesworld
.org/article/san-francisco-marriott-workers-celebrate-new-contract/*; Nancy Hagans,
"Winning the Impossible: The Power of a Nurses' Strike," Medical News,
February 6, 2023, *https://www.medpagetoday.com/opinion/second-opinions/102975
#:~:text=This%20January%2C%207%2C000%20members%20of,York%20
City's%20largest%20hospital%20networks*.

12. Farida Jhabvala Romero, "Oakland Rockridge Trader Joe's Workers Vote to
Unionize amid Unfair Labor Practices Complaints," KQED, April 21, 2023,
*https://www.kqed.org/news/11947282/oakland-rockridge-trader-joes-workers-vote-to
-unionize-amid-unfair-labor-practices-complaints*.

13. Trader Joe's United Webstore, n.d., *https://store.traderjoesunited.org/*.

14. ILR Labor Action Tracker, n.d., *https://striketracker.ilr.cornell.edu/*.

15. "Wage Theft Costs American Workers as Much as $50 Billion a Year," Eco-
nomic Policy Institute, September 11, 2014, *https://www.epi.org/press/wage-theft
-costs-american-workers-50-billion/*.

16. Rodrigo Camarena, interview with the author, June 20, 2023.

17. Annette Bernhardt, Ruth Milkman, and Nik Theodore, "Broken Laws,
Unprotected Workers: Violations of Employment and Labor Laws in

America's Cities," National Employment Law Project, September 21, 2009, *https://www.nelp.org/publication/broken-laws-unprotected-workers-violations-of-employment-and-labor-laws-in-americas-cities/*.

18. "Press Release: Justicia Lab Launches ¡Reclamo!, the Most Comprehensive Platform to Date to Help Immigrant Workers Fight Back against Wage Theft," Justicia Lab, May 16, 2023, *https://www.justicialab.org/blog/justicia-lab-launches-reclamo-the-most-comprehensive-platform-to-date-to-help-immigrant-workers-fight-back-against-wage-theft*.

19. Emily Nonko, "A New Digital Legal Tool Helps Immigrant Workers Reclaim Their Stolen Wages," Next City, May 26, 2023, *https://nextcity.org/features/a-new-digital-legal-tool-helps-immigrant-workers-reclaim-their-stolen-wages?utm_source=Next%2BCity%2BNewsletter&utm_campaign=22a25ed70b*.

20. Jessica Gordon Nembhard, *Collective Courage: A History of African American Cooperative Economic Thought and Practice* (University Park: Pennsylvania State University Press, 2014).

21. Renée Darline Roden, "In a Violent Economy, People of Faith Try Cooperatives," Sojourners, December 7, 2022, *https://sojo.net/articles/violent-economy-people-faith-try-cooperatives*.

22. "The Case for Employee Ownership," Project Equity, May 2020, *https://project-equity.org/publication/case-for-employee-ownership/#:~:text=FULL%20PUBLICATION-,Download%20Report,-EXECUTIVE%20SUMMARY*.

23. "Employee Ownership and Economic Well Being," National Center for Employee Ownership, *https://www.ownershipeconomy.org/*.

24. Gene Marks, "Why Giving Your Employees a Piece of the PIE Could Boost Your Business," *The Guardian*, May 22, 2022, *https://www.theguardian.com/business/2022/may/22/employee-shares-stocks-us-small-business*.

25. Tricia Hersey, *Rest Is Resistance: A Manifesto* (New York: Little, Brown Spark, 2022).

Conclusion

1. Trista Harris, *Future Good: How to Use Futurism to Save the World* (Minneapolis: Wise Ink Creative Publishing, 2020).

2. Octavia E. Butler, *Parable of the Sower* (Newburgh, NY: Thornwillow Press, 1993).

ACKNOWLEDGMENTS

I could fill a whole 'nother book with my gratitude alone. Here's a very abbreviated version.

Thank you to Steve Pierisanti and the Berrett-Koehler team for believing in this Playbook and taking a chance on me as a first-time author.

Thank you to Deb Nelson, who in so many ways helped make this book possible, including by holding the magical container of the Just Economy Institute. JEI blessed me with a community of beloveds on and beyond Paicines Ranch—Tina Beck, Akaya Windwood, Esther Park, Maddy Clark, Abella Glorfield, Allison Kelly, Amrita Wassan, Ashley Clark, Benjamin J. Vann, Caesaré Assad, Caitlin Duffy, Christine Reyes, David Estrada, Eileen Egan, Jessyca Dudley, Jocelyn Wong, Julia Dundorf, Justin Alfond, Kiley Arroyo, Kyle Rudzinski, Lina Shalabi, Liza Siegler, Meg Boucher, Michelle Maryns, Monica Munn, Stephone Coward, Sydney Fang, Vanessa Huang, Wayne Miranda, and the whole alumni community. Special thanks to Addy Lord for being a brilliant connector, Ariel Brooks for being a framework queen, and David Kenney for your many hours of reading and rereading.

Thank you, Joel and Dana Solomon, for opening your desert home as a writing retreat paradise. Thank you to my colleagues across time and space from Candide Group—including but not limited to Aner Ben-Ami, Morgan Simon, Patricia McCarthy, Hope Newsome, Leslie Lindo, Lynne Hoey, starkey baker, Laurika Harris-Kaye, Kim Haywood, and Leticia Corona. And thank you to the professors who opened my world to so many new possibilities: Nina Johnson, Ron Tarver, Sa'ed Atshan, and Lee Smithey, to name just a few.

The words you're holding today have the loving fingerprints of draft readers including Abena Asare, Adrianna Berring, Donovan Ervin,

Johann Klaassen, Jenny Kassan, Joel Redmon, Jezra Kaye, Kim Pate, and Jhana Valentine. Co-conspirators and sage-advice-givers throughout the years of book development have included Emma Guttman-Slater, Tanay Tatum-Edwards, Jordan Sanchez, Lee Kravetz, Mal Warwick, and more. I wouldn't have had the confidence to keep going on this project without early financial support from loving friends and strangers, as well as grants from *Teen Vogue*, Omidyar Network, and more.

I'm lucky every day to be the daughter of Faith and Amin; to be the granddaughter of Francine and Charlie, Roashan Ara and Molla Abdul; and to be (officially) joining the Wheeler family. The universe also definitely made up for my only-childness by giving me some incredible sisters, including Nigeria Talley, Zoya Khan, Samira Saunders, Maya Minhas, and Asuka Wantanabe.

Jo and Smokey, you can't read because you are dogs, but you are two of the best things to ever happen to me. Thank you for humbling me on the daily and reminding me to step away from the silly computer and go outside.

Chase, I don't have sufficient words (only endless tears) to sum up what your support every step of the way on this book has meant to me. Thanks for being the love of my life.

To everyone who sat down with me for an interview: thank you for trusting me to steward your stories. And the organizers connecting the dots between finance and liberation and popular education that haven't yet been mentioned in this book: I see you. Center for Economic Democracy, Beautiful Trouble, Dissenters, Majority Rising, Justice Funders, Third Act, The Guild, Boston Ujima Project, The Center for Popular Democracy, Slow Factory, Wealth Reclamation Academy of Practitioners, Solidaire Network, Common Future, Intersectional Environmentalist, and wow, so many more.

It's hard not to be hopeful in the presence of so much badass momentum.

INDEX

ABOUT THE AUTHOR

 Jasmine Rashid has always believed in people power. It's why in elementary school, she organized car washes outside her parents' home to raise money for endangered manatees. And why in high school, she spent her afterschool hours hosting a student club to discuss social issues. And why, when she had the opportunity to go away to college, she found herself studying, writing about, and participating in movement activism and liberatory campaigns.

Jasmine's passion for economic and racial justice is rooted in her experience navigating the de facto segregated, working-class-to-middle-class suburbs of Long Island, New York. Born in 1996 and growing up as the only child of a Bangladeshi immigrant father working in finance and a Czech Italian American mother working in eldercare (among a million other things), Jasmine was intimately attuned to manmade inequalities under capitalism before she quite had the language for it. She would later return to New York to intern for organizations like ERASE Racism and Human Rights Watch, and organize, alongside childhood friends, the largest known protest for racial justice in her hometown's history.

At Swarthmore College, she special-majored in Peace and Conflict Studies after realizing she couldn't make it through Econ 101 without wanting to talk about people and power. Her scholarship included research cases of international nonviolent social movements, multimedia art exploring human resilience from Philadelphia to Palestine, and policy papers co-created with incarcerated students of Chester State Prison. Her senior thesis, "Bearing Witness: Strategic Human Rights Media of the Rohingya Crisis," won special recognition from the college. Outside of class, she spent a lot of her time running a collaborative zine for students of color, working at the Lang Center for Civic and Social Responsibility, writing for the student newspaper, and reading bell hooks.

Jasmine spent the summer after college in Atlanta, Georgia, exploring civil rights as a Congressman John Lewis Fellow through the Humanity in Action network. Soon after—as the Trump administration was ramping up detention of migrants and separating children from their families—she began working with grassroots partners under the coalition banner #FamiliesBelongTogether. Their campaign strategy focused on putting public pressure on the big banks financing private prison facilities, where migrants were held under inhumane conditions. By 2021, over $2 billion in financial ties to the industry had been cut.

While working on this divestment campaign, Jasmine also entered the other side of the equation: impact investing. She moved to Oakland, California, to join the registered investment advisory firm Candide Group, helping investors flow millions of dollars in investments to predominately women- and people of color–led social justice–focused companies, funds, and organizations. Her early contributions included researching and writing for Forbes.com about the intersection of money and justice. Today, she is Candide Group's director of impact, focused on ecosystem building, investment diligence, and storytelling.

The Financial Activist Playbook came about from a desire to bring everyday people into the conversation about co-creating the next economy. Working daily with financial professionals, wealth holders, and movement organizers, Jasmine tended to the book idea as a fellow with the Just Economy Institute, which is dedicated to bringing together financial activists to shift the flow of capital and power. As part of her research process, she also became certified as a Trauma of Money method practitioner and began hosting "Financial Activist 101" workshops for organizations and community groups.

The Financial Activist Playbook is her first book, and she hopes it empowers readers to own their role in reclaiming wealth and collective well-being for years to come.

Jasmine lives lovingly in Oakland, California, with her fiancé, Chase, and their dogs, Josephine (like Josephine Baker) and Smokey (like from the movie *Friday*). You can visit her website at *JasmineRashid.com*.

Dear reader,

Thank you for picking up this book and welcome to the worldwide BK community! You're joining a special group of people who have come together to create positive change in their lives, organizations, and communities.

What's BK all about?

Our mission is to connect people and ideas to create a world that works for all.

Why? Our communities, organizations, and lives get bogged down by old paradigms of self-interest, exclusion, hierarchy, and privilege. But we believe that can change. That's why we seek the leading experts on these challenges—and share their actionable ideas with you.

A welcome gift

To help you get started, we'd like to offer you a **free copy** of one of our bestselling ebooks:

www.bkconnection.com/welcome

When you claim your **free ebook**, you'll also be subscribed to our blog.

Our freshest insights

Access the best new tools and ideas for leaders at all levels on our blog at ideas.bkconnection.com.

Sincerely,

Your friends at Berrett-Koehler

Certified

Corporation